Work and Wealth in Scripture

Work and Wealth in Scripture

How to Grow, Prosper, and Work as a Christian

Lawrence A. Clayton

RESOURCE *Publications* · Eugene, Oregon

WORK AND WEALTH IN SCRIPTURE
How to Grow, Prosper, and Work as a Christian

Resource Publications
An Imprint of Wipf and Stock Publishers
199 W. 8th Ave., Suite 3
Eugene, OR 97401

www.wipfandstock.com

ISBN 13: 978-1-62032-256-7

Manufactured in the U.S.A.   02/05/2015

This book is dedicated to my friends in the Tuscaloosa County, Alabama, Jail Ministry. There are too many to name all.

I have been going into the jail on Tuesday nights since a friend of mine, Carlton McDaniel (now gone), asked me in 2000 to join him to minister to a Hispanic prisoner, Joaquín Gutiérrez, since I speak Spanish. I have been going in ever since. I have met hundreds of men and women who go into the jail to minister to the prisoners and share the story and promise of Jesus Christ with all of them.

Thousands have accepted Jesus in the jail due to these devoted ministers who bring a message of peace, reconciliation, forgiveness, and the promise of a new life to so many. It is my privilege to share this ministry with you and I hope this little book will help us all in our witness to all in need.

"For the love of money is a root of all kinds of evil. Some people, eager for money, have wandered from the faith and pierced themselves with many griefs" (1 Tim 6:10).

"What good will it be for someone to gain the whole world, yet forfeit their soul? Or what can anyone give in exchange for their soul?" (Matt 16:26).

"If you want to know what God thinks of money, just look at the people he gave it to." Dorothy Parker

"I believe in Christianity as I believe that the Sun has risen: not only because I see it, but because by it I see everything else." C. S. Lewis

Contents

Preface

THIS PREFACE IS REALLY more of a short note on the approach we took in writing this book. I originally intended just to follow Scripture and use the passages, from Genesis to Revelation, on wealth and work. There is little ambiguity in most of those passages—many of which you will see below—although some are perhaps surprisingly realistic, if you haven't read them before, in describing and analyzing the human condition.

As I deepened and widened my search pattern over the months and years, I recognized the immense amount of intelligent, some truly gifted, thought given to the subject over the centuries by my predecessors, mostly, but not all, Christian intellectuals, theologians, historians, philosophers, sociologists, and, in sum, even natural scientists and mathematicians have contributed.

Luckily for me, others such as, for example, Edmund Morgan in his *The Puritan Dilemma: The Story of John Winthrop* and Max Weber in his *The Protestant Ethic and the Spirit of Capitalism*, have worked the ground and there is much to harvest for workers like me.[1] Some of it is immensely complex, problematic, and theoretical, such as the framework and underpinnings of a work like Weber's, whose book first appeared in 1905 and is considered a modern standard by the acknowledged founder of modern sociology. Others, like Morgan's, which was first published in 1958, are, conversely, immensely accessible to the layman. Morgan does not reduce the profound thinking and scholarship of the early Puritans to something simplistic, but rather he takes some things complex—like the struggle to understand how wealth should be handled in the seventeenth century world of the Puritans—and writes about those subjects lucidly and cogently, not losing his readers to the arcane, recondite, and just as often hopelessly contradictory, arguments of intellectuals at sea in the fascinating world of ideas and theories. There is a place for that, but not in this

---

1. Morgan , *The Puritan Dilemma*; Weber, *The Protestant Ethic.*

book, although we will plunge into this world occasionally to ensure that our understanding of what Scripture says about wealth and work is given the proper historical context. Or, in other words, we occasionally dip into this rich literature produced over the centuries, by a vast array of Christian theologians and evangelists across time, such as St. Thomas Aquinas, Erasmus of Rotterdam, and Billy Graham, for example, to see what they have said on the subject. I know some of you may be raising your eyebrows at throwing Billy Graham in with St. Thomas Aquinas, the most popular crusading evangelist of twentieth-century America with probably the deepest thinker in the history of the church (St. Augustine of Hippo supporters will no doubt challenge that interpretation), but I did not want us to steer clear of, or avoid, the truth where or when it was written or spoken.

We have undoubtedly missed many Christian thinkers and activists in this short survey. That's where Scripture has kept us on track. I have turned to it often for the obvious reason—but the obvious needs to be stated—that it is *only* in Scripture where the reader will find the undefiled, no-spin truth, on the subjects of wealth and work. Other cultures and other religions throughout time, from when writing first developed to the newest social media today, undoubtedly contain much on the same subjects and I in no way deny their validity to their followers. However, I am a Christian and Christians firmly believe what Jesus Christ taught us, when Jesus answered, "I am the way and the truth and the life. No one comes to the Father except through me."[2]

With those caveats having been expressed, join me in this little journey and get ready to be jolted a bit along the way. What great trips do you remember? The ones where nothing happened and you had smooth sailing or driving or flying all along the way? Or the ones that surprised and tumbled you, frightened you out of your wits, called upon resources you did not know you had, taught you how to survive and get along, creating memories that will last a lifetime? I can't promise you all that, but I will promise a bucketful of good thinking—all scriptural—that will give you a new light by which to see each day.

2. John 14:6

Acknowledgments

A LOT OF PEOPLE, mostly unnamed since there are many, contributed to my Christian walk that led to this book. But there is one who stands out, not because she is my wife and I need to butter her up, but because she introduced me to a side of Christianity that I must admit I knew little about: the Spirit-filled life.

Louise taught me about the Holy Spirit and the wonderful work he does in our lives, how to access him and how to bring him into one's life as friend, comforter, and counselor.

She introduced me to other elements of my walk, how to do so in faith, how to claim God's gifts and provisions for each and all of us, how to live, in fact, in God's will.

As I moved into the flinty subjects of work and wealth in our lives, I was able to do so with the great and comforting conviction that the core of truth with respect to each of those was revealed in Scripture. So, thanks "Mama," it is a great journey you launched me on and I acknowledge it with love and thanks.

All errors of fact and judgment that have survived in this book are mine and mine alone, and I exempt my wife and all my friends—including pastors, priests, ministers, and brothers in the Lord—from sharing the bad with the good.

Introduction

THIS IS DECIDEDLY AN opinion book.

It is about the Christian matrix of our modern civilization, focusing more narrowly on wealth and work.

It is largely driven by Scripture.

The themes in this book are wealth, or riches, and work, and how the Bible instructs us.

Taken together—wealth and work—Scripture addresses most of our failings and strengths, from greed and pride to charity and love of one's neighbor.

The basic premise is there always has been an immense amount of soul searching on what is right and wrong with America. Even during the times of plenty and apparent prosperity, such as the Roaring Twenties, people thought deeply about the significance of their materials and working lives in the light of Scripture.

The issues have always ranged the gamut from the political ideology and organization of the country, to our role in the world, to the relations between church and state.

Today, each reader can add her own set of issues that are often contentious and divisive, from the greed of Wall Street to what to do about illegal immigrants.

This book offers and summarizes, through direct references to Scripture, the *foundational* truths related to wealth and work in the Bible.

There are, of courses, other sources of opinions and knowledge, sometimes masquerading as wisdom. We will return to this theme below, but suffice it to mention for now that true wisdom comes only from God, while knowledge is largely man-made. We need both, but we also need to be very aware of their sources. When you are very thirsty and see a bubbling spring of apparently cool, fresh water, you better be sure you know its sources. A babbling brook (or babbling know-it-all) may be coming off freshly melted snow from the mountains above, but there may some very fancy homes on up the hills whose septic tanks are leaking because a contractor played loose with the rules to increase his profit.

We read newspaper columnists pontificating on everything under the sun, politicians in Washington committee rooms grilling bankers, stock brokers, and insurance executives, tongue lashing them for greed or incompetence or both. Television journalists—of the left and right—jump all over those very same Republican and Democrat politicians for bringing on catastrophes by their ideologies and actions, and at times all we hear are accusations, loud words, angry people, trying to cope from their basis of human knowledge.

Our standard of living appears to be falling for far too many in a "land of plenty and opportunity," a godless culture undermines values and morality and even nature—global warming (or not) and the concomitant wild fluctuations in weather patterns—appear to make a mockery of what was once predictable and dependable.

People want answers. Let me suggest where they are: in the Bible.

I am not saying that Christianity has all the answers. Other great faiths and streams of thinking exist in the world outside of Christianity. Christianity is, after all, an offshoot of the tree of Judaism, and even Islam's roots are in the Old Testament as well.

But most of the great wisdom on wealth is in the Bible. You will find some in other places, but the wisdom on how to deal with wealth is in the Bible.

I'm not talking about how to invest your money, how to make it, or even how to save it. Many of you have already figured out how you lose it. You can read and study all of those strategies and analyses.

We live, after all, in the greatest free economy the world has ever seen, where capitalism and freedom has produced a cornucopia of wealth, a bounty of living. Self-help books, colleges of business, tax codes and laws, education, enterprise, competition, the law of supply and demand, invention and its rewards, all these go into the stew of a great pot of gold and material advancement.

Wealth seems to be our astrological sign.

Who can argue that penicillin, automobiles, the computer, and a standard of living unsurpassed in the history of man has not been good? We have everything, and at the basis of it is the accumulation of capital—money—and how we spend it and invest it.

But somehow it doesn't bring us joy or happiness in the long run.

Something is missing. And that something is a reason to live beyond ourselves.

What I am directing you to in this little book is that if you think making and accumulating money dominates your life (be honest here), you've missed it. Your relationship with God, more specifically your relationship with Jesus Christ, is going to produce the true joy and happiness God intended for us all.

How to do this? What do I need to do? Where do I find how to do it?

And, equally important, we are *not* going to address your relationship with your God across the board, from Adam to Zebediah.[3] We are focusing rather narrowly on work and wealth as two aspects of your relationship. But you will discover as you read and study that, although superficially narrow—just three little words, *work and wealth*—they represent a large window into your Christian walk. Manage these two, and then move forward into salvation, faith, forgiveness, and all the rest.

If you are a Christian, deep into Scripture and practicing your faith, you're not going to find anything totally new in this book. But I have packaged it for you just like a new gift.

You know the truth. But we need to read and meditate and practice it every day of our lives. You will find in this book a reaffirmation of what you know, perhaps a refocusing, a rekindling of something that has gone latent or grown dim in your life, beset and buffeted by the trials of living.

The bright light of truth may have dimmed like the candle gutting, or a flashlight with spent batteries, just signaling with a dim glow that it is about to go out.

We need to be renewed constantly to the word of God.

When Thomas Jefferson wrote the Declaration of Independence he was so steeped in the classics and in the "modern" thinking about a people and their unspoken, but well understood, "contract" or compact with their rulers, that all who read the Declaration found it immediately easy to understand.

If you were a patriot and agreed with Jefferson, it confirmed your determination to break with a tyrannical King and Parliament. Conversely, if you were a loyalist, the Declaration was as an outrageous act of treason and disloyalty against the same King and Parliament.

In other words, the package or book you are opening will either confirm you in your convictions on how to fit money and work in your life, or

---

3. The father of the apostles John and James for those of you curious. Zebadiah means "gift of Jehovah," most appropriately for our book.

you will find this book simple-minded, an unrealistic code of conduct totally at odds with the world, a chimera of a Christian whose principles—if followed—will lead to poverty and bankruptcy in the "real" world.

But if you are unhappy and frustrated, or believing for something better from God but not quite sure how to access it, then read on. Give it a try. Trade despair, frustration, ignorance, and fear for trust and security.

If you are a so-so Christian, then you need to read on past this introduction and get into the meat of the message. I am not so vain as to write something outrageous such as "this is the most important message you will ever receive in your life," but it is one that shows you how to build a solid foundation for joy and fulfillment, regardless of the circumstances surrounding you.

And if you are not sure of what you are reading, but just picked this book up to browse, and have gotten this far, then take a chance. Be a gambler. Make a deliberate choice to keep reading. You are, after all, endowed by God with free will.

Make the right choice. Join with me in this cruise—not through the Caribbean, but through the Bible—and see where it takes you.

You may be surprised to learn what I have learned over the years of studying Scripture, especially when it gets down to the nitty-gritty—what's in my wallet and bank account and how I handle it. At the end of the last chapter—but hopefully before that—you will have a roadmap, a God-given set of GPS style instructions on how to get from here to there.

How to get from being a slave to wealth to a truly free man.

How might the media go about this? To get us in the mood, let your imagination go outside the box for minute. Turn to the next chapter. Close your eyes for a second or two and imagine "The Interview."

1

The Interview

ONE MORNING IN THE spring of 2012, while in a half-dream, waiting for 5 a.m., to finally roll around so I could get out of bed, something came to mind.

Actually I can get out of bed anytime I feel like, but as I get older and require less sleep, I kept getting out of bed to work and putter around the house earlier and earlier, or, in the hot summertime where I live (Alabama) to go for an occasional long walk.

I was finally getting up before dawn, and, I thought, "This is crazy! I'm like a crazy, eccentric old coot! Do not get up before dawn!"

So, I was waiting for about 5 a.m., when the earliest light of dawn begins to push away the shadows of night—at least during Daylight Savings Time—and finally, after tossing and turning and repeated looks at the clock, it was 5 a.m.! I leaped out of bed with my half-dream still intact.

I was trying to determine how to open the book. How to catch your attention.

Why not open with a conversation, an interview, I thought. Even better, what about an interview with Jesus, or with Jesus and the Apostle Paul, in which questions are asked and answered, kind of in a dialogue form. Just like CNN or Fox.

Of course, some may think of this as sacrilegious, way too light for such as serious subject as religion, and I don't have one of those striking Fox News blondes with ample bosoms and long legs, revealed so well with short skirts, to entertain you, but why not.

Jesus was a real guy, a real person, and while he was serious I suspect he had a sense of humor not always revealed in the four Gospels that made it into the New Testament.

And to keep it entertaining, all the time with the secret agenda of actually learning something useful, we will set it up so there are two interviewers, one from Fox and one from PBS, representing broadly different points of view.

The subject is work and wealth in Scripture. What *does* the Bible say? Let's see how this works.

"This evening," the master of ceremonies [hereafter MC] said, "we have two representatives of the media interviewing two very prominent people in the Christian movement: Jesus Christ, certainly the acknowledged founder of Christianity, and the Apostle Paul, the man who did more to interpret Jesus for the early followers of the church."

"Welcome Jesus and Paul. Thanks for being with us."

Jesus and Paul nodded from where they sat behind the impressive half-round table where the participants were seated. They were wired by the sound technicians with hidden mikes beneath their robes.

"And thanks Jerry Gonzalez-Smith from Fox news," and the MC nodded in the direction of the blonde, "and to Steve Cantor from PBS for joining us this evening." Both Fox and PBS nodded.

"We have asked Jerry and Steve to address the subjects of work and wealth in Scripture, but will allow them some flexibility in their questions since we don't always have such prominent guests to interview.

"So without further ado I will ask our interviewers to begin with their questions, and I'll ask them to begin in alphabetical order. So Fox, you are first."

Fox: "What do you attribute the success of Christianity to?"

Jesus: "Well Ms. Fox who were you addressing that question to? Myself or my good friend here the Apostle Paul?"

Fox: "Well let's start with you Mr. Christ, or may I call you Jesus without any due disrespect?"

Jesus: "Oh just call me Jesus. All my friends do."

Fox: "Thank you, Jesus."

Jesus: "I think the success of our endeavor comes from obedience to our father, the Lord God. As you know—or perhaps you don't know since I know journalists have a very busy agenda—our Father sent me as a messenger, properly called the Messiah, over 2000 years ago to offer man forgiveness and salvation for his sins."

Fox: "Sure, I was raised as a Southern Baptist and remember a lot from Sunday school, although I must admit to not being very attentive with sermons."

Jesus smiled beatifically.

Jesus: "Well that's good Ms. Fox. You know the basics, which a lot of people do—and I might add for the audience that there are more Christians in the world today than any other religion—but the problem seems to be with many that even though they know the rules they don't always obey the rules."

Fox: "Yes, yes kind of like staying under the speed limit on the interstate or sliding through a red light at the intersection. We all do it."

Jesus: "Yes, very good Jerry that's a nice analogy. In fact, I teach in parables which are kind of like analogies. But slipping through a red light doesn't always produce a grievous accident with injuries and death."

Fox: "Yes of course I see that Jesus. The rules your father showed you to show us have bigger consequences. But, returning to my question . . ."

Jesus: "Yes of course, what do we attribute this success of Christianity to? It basically boils down, Ms. Fox, to people wanting to be in a good relationship with their Father, my Father, and me, for I speak for and have authority from my Father. And many blessings will issue from obedience to me and those blessings are both here on earth and in the life that will come after death."

Fox: "And Paul—I may call you Paul I hope—what can you add to the question: why has Christianity been so successful?"

Paul: "Of course Ms. Fox, you may call me Paul. By the way, Jerry, do you have any Jewish ancestors?"

Fox: "Pardon?"

Paul: "Never mind Jerry, just curious since as you may know, but probably don't, that all Christians are descendants of Jews."

Fox: "Ok. And the question?"

Paul: "Well, the reason Christianity has been, and continues to be, so successful is fairly simple," Paul said, but seriously, not warmly like Jesus. "As my Lord Jesus said," Paul started, with a nod towards Jesus, "it comes down to obedience to the Word."

Fox: "The word?"

Paul: "The Word of God, or Scripture, or the writings in the Bible, especially the letters I wrote to the various Christians scattered in churches across Asia and Greece. It all is really very simple."

Fox: "Simple?"

Paul: "Oh, we can make it complicated, bring in the theologians, pundits, cynics, and others who can take a simple idea and turn it into an exceedingly complicated matter. Christians and religious people have tended to do that over the centuries."

Fox: "Hmmm, I seem to remember from Sunday school a letter you wrote to the Romans which was like Greek to me."

Paul: "Well I wrote it in Greek."

Fox: "No, that's not what I mean!"

Paul: "Well, if you read the letter to the Romans, then perhaps you recall from there the answer to your question."

Fox: "Which is?"

Paul: "The question, or the answer?"

Fox: "The answer please, Paul."

Paul: "Christianity is successful as a religion because it is the only way to God."

Fox: "That's it?"

Paul: "Yep."

MC: "Yes, well, let's give PBS a chance to get into this discussion. PBS represented here today by Steve Cantor."

PBS: "Thank you. [Turning to Jesus], Jesus, I've often wondered why God asked you to go to the cross is such a grizzly, painful death when God is omnipotent and could have done anything he wanted, including saving humankind."

Jesus: "Wow, you've been doing your homework, Steve!"

PBS: "Thank you, Jesus."

Jesus: "I don't think I can answer that one as simply as my friend Paul here."

PBS: "But you do have an answer?"

Jesus: "Of course. It has to do with a lot of things, including obedience, disobedience, free will, substitutionary sacrifice, and my Father's determination to make all this comprehensible to humankind."

PBS: "Which is to say, or, in other words?"

Jesus: "God sent me, as human being, to undo the disobedience of Adam and Eve in the beginning of time."

PBS: "I understand. They disobeyed and ate the apple."

Jesus: "And?"

PBS: "And so somehow or another their sin was passed on to us."

Jesus: "Right! And the wages of sin are . . ."

PBS: "Death."

Jesus: "Right again, Steve. You're a good study."

PBS: "Wikipedia, Jesus. I try to do my homework."

Jesus: "And so you have the answer."

PBS: "I, I am following the thread Jesus, but haven't reached the answer. That's why I asked you."

Jesus: "Good journalist that you are! Stay with it! So, the answer is that if all humankind, from Adam and Eve on, are born into sin, and sin leads to eternal death, or separation from God, to lift this eternal condemnation off of man—sorry, humankind—God sent his son—me—to die a substitutionary death and by doing so lift the burden of sin off of you, humankind."

PBS: "But why didn't God just do it with his great power? Instead he condemned you to a terrible death?"

Jesus: "Because sin came in through a man, and it had to be removed, or expiated, by a man. Recall ,Steve, I came to earth as both man and the Son of God."

A long pause ensued, both PBS and Fox reporters scribbling away on their notepads in front of them. The MC stepped in.

MC: So, Steve, Jerry, could we turn to the issue at hand, work and wealth in the Bible? Jerry, could you lead off?

Fox looked up from her notepad, and turned to Jesus.

Fox: "Why do you think, Jesus, that this show picked the twin themes of work and wealth in the Bible for the interview? After all, aren't there more important issues in the Bible? And we can't always count on having you two to interview!"

Jesus: "You remind me of the Pharisee, Jerry, who asked me to summarize all the laws."

Fox: "But you did it I remember, although I don't remember exactly what you said."

Jesus: [Flipping through the iPad on his podium rapidly] "Here it is. My apostle and friend Matthew recorded it in that nice biography he wrote about me. In your Bible it is in the 22nd chapter of Matthew, beginning with verse 37 "You shall love the Lord your God with all your heart and with all your soul and with all your mind."

Fox: "But I remember there was more to it, wasn't there?"

Jesus: "Wow, a quick study you are, girl."

Fox smiled, thinking, "I'm one up on PBS."

Jesus: "That was the great and first commandment that I told Matthew. Then I added one to round out the answer. And a second is like it: "You shall love your neighbor as yourself."

Fox: "Can you do the same thing with the themes of work and wealth Jesus?"

Jesus: "Sure." I wonder why no one ever asked me that, he thought. "How about this one for wealth, Jerry? My disciple Matthew, again, caught the spirit of the answer in his chapter 16, verse 26: 'For what will it profit a man if he gains the whole world and forfeits his soul?'"

Fox: "What do you mean by "gain the whole world?"

Jesus: "Get rich."

PBS: "And money is the root of all evil," Steve of PBS piped up.

Paul: "Close, but not quite it, Steve. I wrote a letter to my follower Timothy and gave him some good advice on this subject. If I may Jesus," Paul said, looking at Jesus.

Jesus: "But of course, Paul. You speak for me with such power and eloquence."

Paul: [Bowing his head a moment in recognition of the compliment] "So, anyhow, I told Timothy that 'the *love* of money is the root of all evil,' in chapter 6 of my first letter to Timothy, I believe in verse 10."

PBS: "Yes, of course. There *is* a difference, isn't there, Jesus?"

Jesus: "Indeed, Steven. There's nothing wrong with money. See," and Jesus reached into his robe and pulled out a few coins, "even I carry some change around to put in the parking meter."

Fox: "You drove here?"

Jesus: "What'd you expect, Jerry? A flaming chariot down 6th Avenue, dropping me off at your studio as it roars away to hold in a pattern over La Guardia?" Fox just stared at Jesus. "When in Rome . . ." Jesus continued, then paused and Paul finished the phrase.

Paul: ". . . do as the Romans do. But, of course, and I think I can speak for Jesus here, don't do everything the Romans do."[1]

Jesus: "Aha, I knew you had a sense of humor, Paul. Good!"

Jerry/Fox and Steve/PBS looked at each other as Jesus and Paul cut up a bit.

MC: "Well, returning to the twin themes of wealth and work in the Bible."

Jesus: "Yes, of course. Do you all know that I address wealth, gold, money, whatever passes for moola in Scripture more than any other subject?"

Fox: "Really?"

---

1. Paul was executed in Rome! By the Romans of course.

Jesus: "Really. Some people who spend far more time studying the Bible than the guys spent writing it say wealth and prosperity and riches occurs in over 2000 passages."

PBS: "2000 places?"

Jesus: "Well, give or take a few. I'm not a scholar you know. I just spoke a lot and that was used by my friends and followers to write the New Testament. But I think the pedants included the Old Testament, as well as the New in their study."

Fox: "And why is this important?"

Paul: "Because whatever you dwell on Jerry is where your heart is. Or, as Jesus put it, 'No one can serve two masters. Either he will hate the one and love the other, or he will be devoted to the one and despise the other. You cannot serve both God and Money.'"

Jesus: "Matthew sure did a good job of remembering all that!"

Paul: "He did Jesus, he surely did."

MC: "And if wealth is so important to understanding what you taught Jesus, where does work come in? How high or low in the pecking order? Uh, sorry, I'm supposed to MC not ask questions," he added, looking for approval from PBS and Fox, who both nodded their ascent. "Anyhow, let me get us started in that direction."

Fox: "Can I sharpen the question a bit? By what do you think is meant 'work' in the Bible?"

Paul: "If I may Jesus?" Paul started, looking at Jesus.

Jesus: "Sure, Paul. Get us started. You always were a great worker. What *is* the meaning of work in Scripture?"

Paul: "Like so many words, it has many meanings Jerry, Steve," Paul said, directing his answer to the two reporters. They nodded, and kept their pencils at the ready to take a note or two. Even in the high tech world of iPads, iPhones, and mobile devices, most reporters simply could not substitute any of the techie stuff for a notepad and a quick write.

Paul: "Work, of course, is what we do for a living, on one level. I, for example, made my living as a tentmaker."

Steve/PBS: "A what?"

Paul: [Pausing, as if talking to a slow student, or one not listening] "I made tents, you know the things you set up in the Great Smoky National Park when you go camping to keep the water off?"

Jerry/Fox: [Smirking a bit] "He doesn't know what a tent is Paul. He probably has an RV."

Paul: "Ok, good point. Let's say Steve manufactured RVs in Indiana."

Steve: "I do know what a tent is you two. I just didn't hear Paul."

Jesus: "Ok, so Paul was a tentmaker and . . ." Jesus interjected to get the flow going again.

Paul: "Right. I was also a Pharisee, an evangelist, a preacher, a teacher, and a lot of other things, but, to make my living, I made tents."

Steve: "Did you get paid for the other things you did? Don't we pay pastors and preachers today? They always seem to be asking for money on TV."

Paul: "Yes, yes, a man should be compensated for preaching and teaching. It is honest work. But in my time, one had to depend on the gifts of your listeners, and some of the places I preached in were poor or afflicted, so I worked as a tentmaker. Let me be more precise, Steve. I didn't want to be a burden on anyone, and, besides, man is made to work."

Steve: Scribbling rapidly on his notepad, "Man is made to work. Is that it?"

Jesus: "That's part of it, Steve. Work is tied in with our other subject, wealth. If you work, you could get wealthy or rich. If you don't work, you could end up poor and miserable. Those are two ends of what we could call today the 'economic spectrum.'"

Jerry/Fox: "But not everyone who works gets wealthy, and not everyone who is a loafer ends up poor, Jesus."

Jesus: "Good point. It gets a bit more complex, but let's stick to the basics for a moment, then we can deal with the exceptions or 'mitigating factors' as the lawyers would say."

Steve: "Ok. Let's say we accept the premise that being rich is good—we all like a little change in our pockets, right?—and being poor is kind of crappy. Where does work come into the equation if not everyone who works—a tentmaker like Paul here for example—becomes rich, and some, even though they may work hard, never move out from the ranks of the poor."

Jesus: "Now you're catching the nuances, Steve. My ancestors in the Old Testament were pretty honest in appraising the differences between the rich and poor, for example: 'The poor are shunned even by their neighbors, but the rich have many friends.' But they also added 'Better a little with the fear of the Lord than great wealth with turmoil.'[2] What did they mean by this?"

2. Prov 14:20 and 15:16.

Jerry/Fox: "Wealth brings a lot of problems that the poor don't have, I suppose."

Jesus: "Wealth tends to spawn a sense of well-being attributed to riches."

Paul: "And one forgets that true wealth—the love of God—cannot be bought."

Steve: "Okay, okay. But work? Where does this fit into the equation? So far we keep going back to wealth as the source of a lot of things, but work, making tents, interviewing people on TV, where does it fit in?"

Jesus: "Ah, good, Steve. Scripture tended to equate wealth with God's blessings, and the poor as the absence of God's blessings. Or, to put it another way, to be poor was considered a curse put on people by God. So, the goal—at least one goal and maybe not even the most important—was to move away from poverty to wealth."

Jerry and Steve scribbling like mad.

Jesus: [Continuing] "so the sluggard or lazy bones was chastised for contributing to his poverty, while the busy worker gathered about him the fruits of his labor and was blessed. Let's take another page from a book written by more of my ancestors. 'Go to the ant, you sluggard; consider its ways and be wise! It has no commander, no overseer or ruler, yet it stores its provisions in summer and gathers its food at harvest.' And, even more to the point: "How long will you lie there, you sluggard? When will you get up from your sleep? A little sleep, a little slumber, a little folding of the hands to rest—and poverty will come on you like a thief and scarcity like an armed man."[3]

Jerry/Fox: "Sounds like work was the source of wealth *or* poverty. Kind of simplistic."

Paul: "But scriptural, and, if you examine it in more detail, Jerry, in the main, true."

Steve/PBS: "Like how Paul?"

Paul: "Like what I wrote to the Galatians, Steve. 'A man reaps what he sows.' You don't sow, you don't reap, you become poor. You do sow, you reap and you have plenty."

Jesus: "Paul said a bit more to the Galatians, didn't you, Paul?"

Paul: "Indeed Jesus. I added something more important than riches or impoverishment here on earth. 'Whoever sows to please their flesh, from

3. Prov 6:6–11.

the flesh will reap destruction; whoever sows to please the Spirit, from the Spirit will reap eternal life.'"[4]

Jerry/Fox: "So work has a spiritual meaning too? You use sowing as a synonym for work, right?"

Paul: "Right, Jerry, the two are intersecting all the time. The earthly and the spiritual."

Steve/PBS: "Can you explain that, Paul."

Paul: "Sure, my ancestors put it pretty plainly in Proverbs. For example, 'Do not love sleep or you will grow poor; stay awake and you will have food to spare.' Then, moving more into the larger world of knowledge and wisdom, 'Gold there is, and rubies in abundance, but lips that speak knowledge are a rare jewel.'"[5]

Jerry/Fox: "So work and wealth are directly related? You work, and get wealth, don't work, and stay poor? One is blessed and the other cursed by God?"

Jesus: "You are now thinking outside the box, Jerry. That's great! But we have to be careful we don't confuse work with works."

Steve/PBS: "Did you say work and works, with an 's' Jesus? What's the difference?"

Jesus: "Well, a bit of semantics here, Steve. Jerry put the two elements together—work and wealth—but came to a wrong conclusion." And then Jesus turned to Jerry, "But not an erroneous conclusion Jerry! Let me explain. Works—with an 's' as Steve caught—can sometimes, in a religious framework, be interpreted as a key to enter my kingdom. In other words, doing good things—works—is equated with acceptance in my kingdom."

Steve/PBS: "Jesus, by 'works,' what do you mean? Like feeding the poor, taking care of the sick?"

Jesus: "Exactly. Work on the other hand—no 's'—is what I expect all my followers to do. Make a living, just like my good friend Paul here did as a tentmaker, even while he answered my call to take my message to the Gentiles."

Paul: "And—if I may Jesus—let's be clear that there is nothing inherently wrong with works. In fact, I wrote my young friend Timothy exactly something along these lines: 'Command those who are rich in this present world not to be arrogant nor to put their hope in wealth, which is so uncertain, but to put their hope in God, who richly provides us with everything

4. Gal 6:7–9.

5. Prov 20:13, 15.

for our enjoyment. Command them to do good, to be rich in good deeds, and to be generous and willing to share. In this way they will lay up treasure for themselves as a firm foundation for the coming age, so that they may take hold of the life that is truly life.'"[6]

Steve/PBS: "So let me see if I got this right. 'Work' and 'works,' with an 's' are two different but related ways to view what a man does with his time and energy."

Jesus: "Right."

Steve/PBS: "Work will produce not only wealth, and we all know *that* is not guaranteed . . ."

Paul: "Right again."

Steve/PBS: [Continuing] ". . . but Scripture does equate the acquisition of wealth, or, loosely, material things and some comfort, as a sign from God that that man is favored."

Jesus: "Yes, the general correlation, if I may get a bit mathematical, is correct between wealth or riches or being well off, whatever you want to call it, and the blessings of my father. That it doesn't always happen that way is, of course, also true."

Steve/PBS: "You can acquire wealth illegally or by force or in some other fashion not consistent with God's rules, right?"

Paul: "And that wealth leads to or is caused by sin, and sin leads to . . ." [and here Paul pauses].

Jerry/Fox: "Death."

Jesus: "Right!"

Jerry/Fox: "It can get complicated."

Paul nodded but said nothing.

Steve/PBS: "And if I can finish, on the other hand works with an 's' is interpreted in Scripture as the doing of 'good' things for one's fellow man, helping the widows, giving to the poor, ministering to the sick, tithing."

Paul: "You got it, Steve. But there's one other element that we need to consider when we consider 'works' and that is faith.

MC: Looking at the big clock on his panel, "I'm afraid we are about to run out of time, and Paul is moving into another orbit on the subject of faith. Thank you Jesus [Jesus nods], Paul [Paul also], Jerry [big smile] and Steve [clipped nod] for joining us tonight."

[And the scene fades to a close.]

6. 1 Tim 6:17–19.

I open my eyes and blink a few times. Was I dreaming, imagining, or simply wondering how to package the subject, having been watching too many talking heads on television, the presidential debates in late 2012 as Mr. Obama and Mr. Romney went at it, an overheated imagination that probably transgressed the boundaries of good sense? Jesus in an interview on Fox TV or PBS radio?

I realize it is the historian in me coming to the fore. Paul and Jesus were real figures in history, real men, who—although extraordinary and, in Jesus' case, unique—lived and talked and worked to bring the truth of God's will to man.

Before we go further, however, I am curious about you, the reader. What do you do? It was a question I posed to someone a few years ago and was I surprised by his answer. This is not a trick question, but one to help us probe a bit into who we are and what we do, and, later, to see how we can line up better with what *God* wants us to be and do.

Questions for Discussion:

- What *is* work? What *is* wealth?
- How real is Jesus to you?
- And, can you give examples?
- What's the difference between work and works?
- What else would you put in this imagined script/interview?

2

What Do You Do?

Heigh-ho, heigh-ho
It's off to work we go
We keep on singing all day long
Heigh-ho
Heigh-ho, heigh-ho
Got to make your troubles go
Well, you keep on singing all day long
Heigh-ho
Heigh-ho, heigh-ho[1]

YEARS AGO I WENT to a black-tie banquet somewhere in Manhattan—the Plaza I seem to remember—where someone like a cabinet-level Secretary of Something or Another was speaking. It was in 1979–1980, so it was probably one of President Jimmy Carter's people.

The table where I sat was sponsored by W. R. Grace & Co., then with headquarters in New York, and really a New York corporate institution dating from the 1860s until it abandoned the "city" and headed south to Florida, like so many New Yorkers over the years. But in the winter of 1979–1980, Grace, with its offices on 42nd Street overlooking Bryant Park behind the New York Public Library, was a big time corporation, and it sponsored tables at big time banquets. I happened to be one of the invited guests, a small-time historian from Alabama with few credentials, but with a borrowed tux and some well-placed friends in the company.

---

1. "Heigh-Ho" is a song from Walt Disney's 1937 animated film *Snow White and the Seven Dwarfs*, written by Frank Churchill (music) and Larry Morey (lyrics). It is sung by the group of seven dwarfs as they work at a mine with diamonds and rubies, and is one of the best-known songs in the film. Thanks to Hugh Whelchel, *How Then Should We Work: Rediscovering the Biblical Doctrine of Work*, who used Heigh-Ho as the epigraph for his book, and reminded me of this wonderful doggerel from the land of Disney many of us grew up in.

Before I get to the amazing encounter I had with someone who represented a value and a point of view so foreign to me as to leave me dumfounded, mouth open, wondering how innocent of the world I really may be, I have to give you some background.

I was thirty-nine at the time, and not so innocent, a Navy veteran, six years living in New Orleans, a traveler across the Americas and Europe, a professor, a PhD, a person who grew up in Lima, Peru and just outside of New York City, and with credentials that on the surface spoke of some cosmopolitan or metropolitan formation. But I wasn't ready for what I heard that night at the banquet, not from the speaker who I forget, but from a fellow diner sitting next to me, in his tux as well, probably owned not borrowed like mine.

I had come to New York in June of 1979 to work for a year at the company headquarters on a history of W. R. Grace & Co. in Latin America. Periodically, the company "bought" a table—usually in some fashionable hotel midtown—when some bigwig was in town, a politico, or some equally prominent speaker with national or international stature. My friend and contact in the company, Dick Moore, would invite me occasionally to these events, and even loaned me his tux.

So it was that one evening, in my black tie outfit, I found myself in some gilded, glistening golden room, probably the Plaza, sitting at a table with eight or ten invited guests of the company, facing a fabulous setting of silver and flowers and other stuff that make people feel important, like name tags, little gifts, and the like. It was a far cry from my near subsistence level of living at my little place in Greenwich Village, but I was content there, and, from my upbringing and life to then (another chapter) felt equally comfortable with the glitter, the rich, and the famous.

As Eisenhower (General and then President Dwight David Eisenhower) once commented on his high stature and prominence in public life, and everyone else, "most of us put our trousers on the same way, every day," as a way of saying that he was just one of us. So, I could be one of them, a secret academic pedant rubbernecking on the rich and famous and powerful. And, I considered myself both social scientist *and* humanist, since as historians we move easily across the aisle separating the "scientists," albeit social, and the artists or humanists who interpret as much as tell about and dissect the world. Here I was, observing, taking note of how wealth and power were demonstrated in the biggest of the Big Apples, when I innocently, to break the ice, asked my neighbor at the table, "What do you do?"

He looked at me as though I'd interrupted something, perhaps thinking a great thought or simply meditating on his salad or the wine being served, or his latest investments, or meeting his mistress at some bistro, or her apartment after the banquet, and said something like, "I facilitate mergers," and returned to his wine or fork. I forget truthfully the exact sequence of events but it was something like that.

I thought about it a second, and continued, the social scientist, "What do you facilitate merging?"

Again, a quizzical look, kind of like some scientist looking at a specimen through his microscope.

"Companies," he said with a shrug, no doubt confused by the rube—me—sitting next to him. What the hell else would I be doing on Wall Street? he must have thought.

"Ah," I said or thought, and following my thread of inquiry, and being polite. "It sounds like a fascinating job," and "How did you get into it?"

Again, the look, now moving from condescending to slightly contemptuous.

"To make money," he answered. "And what do *you* do?"

"I teach history."

That, as near as I can remember, ended our conversation, each one of us turning to other distractions at our table or perhaps the events unfolding at the dais where the speaker was preparing his speech, or maybe just crunching on a carrot from his salad, improving his eyesight, or thinking about where he was and what he proposed to say.

I never forgot my dinner companion's answer to "and what do you do?"

I make money, and I could tell that he enjoyed making money, lots of money, and that making money, getting rich, gaining wealth, was an end in itself for this man. Acquiring wealth to him was not a job but a vocation, like others study law, or medicine, or agronomy, or carpentry, moving on across the scale of the professions to the skills and vocations of our lives.

Back in 1987 Michael Douglas made a movie, *Wall Street*, in which he starred as a ruthless stockbroker whose motto was "greed is good," and the movie paired him against a young, idealistic stockbroker played by Charlie Sheen who had to reconcile the same love for money with his background that stressed other values. I think I must have met one of the models for that movie almost ten years earlier, when that 1979 or 1980 I engaged my fellow diner in that very short conversation at the banquet at the Plaza, or Waldorf, or wherever we sat down in black ties to a sumptuous dinner.

After the banquet I followed my normal routine and headed for the nearest subway stop, in black tie on my way back downtown to my digs in Greenwich Village with other late night straphangers. Nobody paid me the flippest of attention. Black tie, rap, hip hoppers, late night disco denizens, people going to work, people going home, the subway clientele is a mélange of democracy in the city.

I started to pull my bow tie off a I came out of the subway station at Union Square and 14th Street, keeping a weather eye out for the castaways who inhabited that bit of urban space, but turning south to cross the street and head "home." After a few months I felt like that part of the city was indeed my home, albeit a home away from home. And I wondered about my values. Was I so unrealistic and innocent in my views towards riches and wealth? Was that guy I met—even in a grossly exaggerated fashion—closer to the truth of the matter than I? Was that a legitimate "profession"? Make money? Where did the truth of the matter lay?

As I thought about it, so what if you made a lot of money. Years later when I was chairman of the history department at the University of Alabama, where I taught for more than forty years, I would of course occasionally "mentor" my faculty, especially my younger faculty, who were, for the most part, always needing more money for travel, research, writing, all the things we did to avoid getting sacked in a work environment where "publish or perish" was the reigning principle.

My standard answer to their requests, either formal or in informal chats, was, "Okay, Loretta, so what if we had a $5 million dollar gift to give you, what would do with it?"

"No strings attached?"

"No strings attached. $5 million free. Kind of like a MacArthur Grant," I would say, in reference to a very generous, no strings attached, fellowship program that gave money away to those with much promise. Genius grants they are called by some.

"Well," and then they would describe their research program, where they would go, the resources they could reach or tap into, new computers to do the work, the fastest laptop of course, and then what I would ask, "Then what?"

"Well, you said no strings attached. Maybe I could pay off my debts, pay the mortgage, things like that."

"And then if you did all that and say you had about four and a half million left, what would you do?"

The answer was usually in the general category of "Uh, I dunno, maybe give some to charity, like a church you know . . ." and our conversation would trail off.

My point was once you get all this money, what you decide to do with it tells me a lot about you. It's kind of like doing an inventory of how people spend their money or their time. Find out one or the other, or both, and I'll nail you as to who you are.

So, what do you do? Do you just make money? That's not a major, or even a minor, principle or rule in Scripture. Don't confuse working for a living with making money. The Apostle Paul wrote the church at Thessalonica and instructed them on a lot of things, among them warning against idleness. He really jumped on them since he had heard some were loafing, just idle.

"For you yourselves know how you ought to follow our example," he lectured them. "We were not idle when we were with you, nor did we eat anyone's food without paying for it."

And then to make sure they got the message: "On the contrary, we worked night and day, laboring and toiling so that we would not be a burden to any of you. We did this, not because we do not have the right to such help, but in order to offer ourselves as a model for you to imitate."

And he gave them a rule: "The one who is unwilling to work shall not eat."[2]

So, working to Paul was not to make money. Money was simply a medium given in exchange for work. Work, to Paul, was to support himself in his ministry. That was always his priority after his conversion on the road to Damascus. And anyone who was idle or loafing was definitely out of sync with God's rules. "We hear that some among you are idle and disruptive. They are not busy; they are busybodies. Such people we command and urge in the Lord Jesus Christ to settle down and earn the food they eat."

Work for Paul deserved compensation, as was obvious from the above. As was also obvious, Paul was not working to amass wealth. He worked to support his ministry. But he also wrote, this time to the Corinthians, that his ministry itself deserved compensation. In other words, preachers deserved to be supported by those they preach to.

"Don't we have the right to food and drink?" he asked the Corinthians. Didn't he have the right to bring a wife along, "as do the other apostles and the Lord's brothers and Cephas [Peter]?"

2. 2 Thess 3:6–12.

Don't soldiers get paid? Don't those who plant vineyards expect to eat its grapes, drink its wine? "Who tends a flock and does not drink the milk? Whoever plows and threshes should be able to do so in the hope of sharing in the harvest."

Then he really gets personal. "If we have sown spiritual seed among you, is it too much if we reap a material harvest from you?"[3] The answer is, of course, no!

Work is part of life for Paul, and it should be for us as well. It is not an end in itself. Let's be as clear as possible. The goal or objective of any man's life—and we'll dispense with the formalities of politically correct jargon in this book, by man I mean all men, women, and children, of all races and colorations—is to please God. Do that, and God will take care of you.

I am not disclaiming the good feeling that comes from a "job well done." In fact, job satisfaction is high on the ideals of any person's relationship to their work. God himself has a plan of work for you. Jesus told a parable where the servant was rewarded for his good work. "His master replied, 'Well done, good and faithful servant! You have been faithful with a few things; I will put you in charge of many things. Come and share your master's happiness!'"[4]

In his wonderful, poetic, metaphorical style, the Apostle John also addressed work and its end. "Do not work for food that spoils," he admonished, "but for food that endures to eternal life, which the Son of Man will give you."[5] Work, obviously, has a higher end than "making money."

The book of Psalms, perhaps the highest expression of wisdom in the Bible along with the book of Proverbs, addresses work. Read it slowly, and savor it. It will lead us to subjects that follow in other chapters.

> For all can see that the wise die,
> that the foolish and the senseless also perish,
> leaving their wealth to others.
> Their tombs will remain their houses forever,
> their dwellings for endless generations,
> though they had named lands after themselves.
> People, despite their wealth, do not endure;
> they are like the beasts that perish.
> This is the fate of those who trust in themselves,
> and of their followers, who approve their sayings.

3. 1 Cor 9:3–12.

4. Matt 25:23.

5. John 6:27.

They are like sheep and are destined to die;
death will be their shepherd
(but the upright will prevail over them in the morning).
Their forms will decay in the grave,
far from their princely mansions.
But God will redeem me from the realm of the dead;
he will surely take me to himself.
Do not be overawed when others grow rich,
when the splendor of their houses increases;
for they will take nothing with them when they die,
their splendor will not descend with them.
Though while they live they count themselves blessed—
and people praise you when you prosper—
they will join those who have gone before them,
who will never again see the light of life.
People who have wealth but lack understanding
are like the beasts that perish.[6]

Let's back away from the soaring poetry of Psalms for a moment. The next step in our exploration is what do you do with what your job earns? I don't care if you are a stockbroker on Wall Street or a coal miner in West Virginia, or slinging hamburgers at a McDonald's in L.A.

So what do *you* do? And, equally important, what do you do with what you earn?

Part of that answer is determined by what you consider valuable. For that question, let's turn to the next chapter.

Questions for Discussion:

- Was it impolite to ask my banquet companion, "What do you do?"

- Why are teaching history and making money incompatible? Or, are they?

- Why did the Apostle Paul work at tentmaking?

- How important is your work in defining your life?

---

6. Ps 49:10–20.

3

What is Valuable?

Wisdom is a shelter
as money is a shelter,
but the advantage of knowledge is this:
Wisdom preserves those who have it (Eccl 7:12).

What good will it be for someone to gain the whole world, yet forfeit their soul? Or what can anyone give in exchange for their soul? (Matt 16:26).

Command those who are rich in this present world not to be arrogant nor to put their hope in wealth, which is so uncertain, but to put their hope in God, who richly provides us with everything for our enjoyment. Command them to do good, to be rich in good deeds, and to be generous and willing to share. In this way they will lay up treasure for themselves as a firm foundation for the coming age, so that they may take hold of the life that is truly life (1 Tim 6:17–19).

WHICH IS MORE VALUABLE: wealth or wisdom? Be honest. What's your first answer? Not just wealth, but be thinking of money in the bank, investments in blue chip stocks, a car or two or three, something tangible, a great retirement income, secured by unimpeachable sources, your bills paid off, a cabin down by the beach or river, or enough money in the bank to buy anything, and a good job, paying well.

When I sit down at my computer, I have many choices, but the sites I probably visit the most are my online bank accounts to take care of the financial flow of monies in my family, and my Outlook app with all my emails and electronic correspondence. On the other hand, I would say that the *most important*, the *most valuable* site listed in my bookmarks is my

Gateway Bible app where I find and either can read or listen to Scripture on a daily basis.

Now, if I am really honest I *have* to admit that I don't even visit that site on a daily basis. So, according to my way of telling what is important in your/my life—by looking at how I spend my time—you can easily nail me.

How do you spend your time, when it comes to what is valuable in your life, especially as we address the question of wealth?

Scripture tells us, with certainty, that wealth itself is but a measure of things. How many things do you have? How many dollars in your bank account? How many securities with your stock broker or retirement account? Or, conversely, how little of the things that you need to get along do you have? You may have lots of debt—"negative things" let's call them.

"I don't have anything" may be another refrain when we deal with things we have, or don't have. As an old saying goes, with respect to another thing—luck—if I didn't have bad luck I wouldn't have any luck.

Or would you rather have something Scripture says is more valuable— wisdom? Let's make this choice a bit more difficult. Trade in all your things, and mine would have to include my motorcycle, my little airplane, and, let's throw the ones in that I am almost inseparable from, my computers, my iPads, and maybe even two or three of my favorite dogs, throw them all away, or put them in storage for a while (the pets can go to a nice pet hotel), and separate myself from all the things, and just read Scripture, occasionally stepping away to do something kind for someone else. Since the hospital is just around the corner from where I live, go visit some friends in the hospital.

And then, with some of the things you have in the bank, sign up for a mission trip to Uganda or Thailand or Honduras, or, bite the bullet on this one, how about Haiti, where the poorest of the poor live, if by living we can define mere subsistence. Or, if you are really intrepid, head off to South Sudan where Christians are being persecuted, harried, and killed for their faith. Live in a tent. Use an open latrine or outhouse for your business. Take a bath or shower maybe once or twice a week, if you can find water.

"Are you nuts?" you may be saying or thinking.

Your answer to this question is critical. Jesus posed it to the rich young ruler. You remember the story:

> As Jesus started on his way, a man ran up to him and fell on his knees before him. "Good teacher," he asked, "what must I do to inherit eternal life?"

"Why do you call me good?" Jesus answered. "No one is good—except God alone. You know the commandments: 'You shall not murder, you shall not commit adultery, you shall not steal, you shall not give false testimony, you shall not defraud, honor your father and mother.'"

"Teacher," he declared, "all these I have kept since I was a boy."

Jesus looked at him and loved him. "One thing you lack," he said. "Go, sell everything you have and give to the poor, and you will have treasure in heaven. Then come, follow me."

At this the man's face fell. He went away sad, because he had great wealth.

Jesus looked around and said to his disciples, "How hard it is for the rich to enter the kingdom of God!"

The disciples were amazed at his words. But Jesus said again, "Children, how hard it is to enter the kingdom of God! It is easier for a camel to go through the eye of a needle than for someone who is rich to enter the kingdom of God."

The disciples were even more amazed, and said to each other, "Who then can be saved?"

Jesus looked at them and said, "With man this is impossible, but not with God; all things are possible with God."[1]

This is a *hard* lesson for those of us in the modern world, especially in America, surrounded and comforted by things our wealth has provided for us. Let's be honest. They *are* valuable to us, not because we are inherently more sinful than any other people who have less (take Haitians just for example to make an extreme comparison), but because God has blessed this nation. But things have become more valuable than wisdom. Remember the question we posed at the beginning the chapter just above. What is valuable to you? In following the path to the answer that Scripture provides, we must do it honestly.

So what is the Bible's answer to the question? Part of it was in Jesus's instructions (above) to the rich young man's question. He must lay aside his worldly wealth and instead seek "treasure in heaven." Jesus knew where the young man's heart was. Where's yours?

Here's one other little bromide that serves a useful purpose, and, although a very honest one, it usually makes just about everyone mad.

1. Mark 10:17–27.

Tell me how you spend your money and I'll tell you what kind of a person you are.

Think about that. I can also tell you what you are thinking most of the day and night. Give me a few minutes with your computer, and I'll tell you where your mind is.

You may say this is a privacy issue. It's none of your business where my wealth is or how I spend my time on the computer. But we are in the truth business in this book, so let's examine the question, "what is valuable?" from different points of view. What about Wall Street for starters?

In the movie *Wall Street*, Michael Douglas plays the role of an unscrupulous corporate raider who noted in perhaps the most famous line in the movie, "greed, for lack of a better word, is good." You may think, well that is the expression of a godless minority in this country, people depraved and driven by simple greed. Or, conversely, you may agree with him, not exactly in such a stark fashion, "greed . . . is good," but as we examine in chapters 4 and 5, especially the latter, greed—when toned down a bit from the raw into something refined—is one of the driving motivations of capitalism, and capitalism is the driving force of success and progress in America. That is, of course, grossly simplistic, and we examine the phenomenon in chapter 5. There are consequences—serious consequences—to greed which is basically antisocial and pretty much ignores your fellow man. And *that* is most assuredly non-Christian.

Matthew cuts to the chase in the answer to the question of what is truly valuable: "What good will it be for someone to gain the whole world, yet forfeit their soul? Or what can anyone give in exchange for their soul?" (Matt 16:26) Matthew is speaking here of our eternal life, what comes after we die. Or, to put it in other words, life on earth is transitory. The life of our soul is eternal, from which there is no return to make things right on earth.

This Christian principle has been examined exhaustively over the ages, sometimes with deep cynicism, such as by Karl Marx, the father of Marxism, who observed that "religion is the opiate of the masses." In other words, rulers lorded it over the great masses of peasants, peons, slaves, and the like by encouraging the church to promise them eternal life if they behaved on earth. And that meant obedience to their rulers and owners. Even Paul preached obeying your rulers, so the church could preach passivity, conformity, and obedience as a scriptural imperative.

In Romans 13, verses 1–7 Paul lays out the rules rather unequivocally "Let everyone be subject to the governing authorities, for there is no authority except that which God has established. The authorities that exist have been established by God." This is pretty straightforward. In Paul's time, he was speaking of Roman authority, established and maintained by Roman legions and governors. If you valued liberty and life, you obeyed Rome. This mandate to obey authority would of course eventually get Christians in trouble in the first three centuries of their existence. If they obeyed their God, they could not also obey, and worship, Rome, or, more specifically, the Roman emperor. If Christians insisted that they could only worship the one true God, and refused to acknowledge publicly that the Roman emperor was divine, then they were considered rebellious. And Paul wrote, "whoever rebels against the authority is rebelling against what God has instituted, and those who do so will bring judgment on themselves."

The mandate to obey rulers has produced a lot of conflict in Christian communities, especially when rulers, and, even more especially, hereditary rulers such as monarchs, kings, emperors, and the like, behaved in a transparently evil fashion. Some were mad, others depraved, others just plain wicked. What then? Do we have the right to disobey rulers? And, by doing so, jeopardize our salvation, which, as Matthew stated, was more important than anything?

Could Christians legitimately challenge authority, disobey the laws of the land? Acts 5:27-29 suggests that, yes, disobedience was a right of Christians, *if* the laws or government contravened or contradicted the will of God: "Having brought the apostles, they made them appear before the Sanhedrin to be questioned by the high priest. 'We gave you strict orders not to teach in this Name,' he said. 'Yet you have filled Jerusalem with your teaching and are determined to make us guilty of this man's blood.' Peter and the other apostles replied: '*We must obey God rather than men!*'" [italics added].

Later, in the mid-twentieth century, Nazi war criminals were put on trial, the major trial taking place at Nuremberg, and were accused, indicted, and condemned of precisely *not* questioning or disobeying instructions to exterminate the Jews, among many horrors committed by Hitler's regime. Their defense was basically, "we were only following orders," or obeying the authority of the government. But the allied justices (English, French, Russian, and American) found them guilty of "crimes against humanity," and, in fact, invoked the higher laws of God over those of man.

We won't pursue this string further, since it leads us away from work and wealth, but the implications for our study are clear. Returning to Jesus and Paul, of what profit would it be to gain the world, and yet forfeit your soul? Indeed, in the very act of "gaining the world," a simple way of saying getting rich, getting things, making wealth for its own sake, one tends to lose track of what *is* important, which is being in the will of God.

One note here, before moving on, lest you get the wrong impression. Being in the will of God does not mean the same thing as being poor or accepting poverty as your lot in life. It means what it says: staying in the will of God. He will then help determine the direction of your life, and your fortune, in accordance with his will *and* the expression of your free will, also a gift from God.

The story of Lazarus is instructive here. We can paraphrase it, but Luke tells it so well that we turn to Luke 16:19–31 (World English Bible):

Now there was a certain rich man, and he was clothed in purple and fine linen, living in luxury every day. A certain beggar, named Lazarus, was laid at his gate, full of sores, and desiring to be fed with the crumbs that fell from the rich man's table. Yes, even the dogs came and licked his sores.[2] It happened that the beggar died, and that he was carried away by the angels to Abraham's bosom. The rich man also died, and was buried. In Hades, he lifted up his eyes, being in torment, and saw Abraham far off, and Lazarus at his bosom. He cried and said, "Father Abraham, have mercy on me, and send Lazarus, that he may dip the tip of his finger in water, and cool my tongue! For I am in anguish in this flame."

But Abraham said, "Son, remember that you, in your lifetime, received your good things, and Lazarus, in the same way, bad things. But now here he is comforted and you are in anguish. Besides all this, between us and you there is a great gulf fixed, that those who

2. Illustration of Lazarus at the rich man's gate by Fyodor Bronnikov, 1886: http://en.wikipedia.org/wiki/Rich_man_and_Lazarus.

want to pass from here to you are not able, and that none may cross over from there to us."

He said, "I ask you therefore, father, that you would send him to my father's house; for I have five brothers, that he may testify to them, so they won't also come into this place of torment."

But Abraham said to him, "They have Moses and the prophets. Let them listen to them."

He said, "No, father Abraham, but if one goes to them from the dead, they will repent."

He said to him, "If they don't listen to Moses and the prophets, neither will they be persuaded if one rises from the dead."

The lesson of this parable, which may be a true story as well, is clear. One decides here on earth how one will spend life in eternity. Charles Dickens took this as his theme in his wonderful novella *A Christmas Carol*, published in 1843. I'll not go over this classic story in any detail but remind you that one of the principal characters was named Ebenezer Scrooge. "Scrooge" has worked its way into the English language to mean someone stingy, cold-hearted, and greedy, whose only thought was how to make and preserve his money. Even Walt Disney incorporated Scrooge into his pantheon of cartoon characters, including such all-time and beloved favorites as Mickey Mouse and Donald Duck. Donald of course had to contend with his equally famous Uncle Scrooge who was almost always depicted surrounded by his money bags and driving Donald nuts with his stinginess.

Dickens' novel recast of the story of Lazarus and the rich man, but the same moral emerged, pointing us as always in this chapter to "what is valuable?" Scrooge is visited from the other world by his dead partner Jacob Marley who warns Scrooge that he will follow Marley into eternal perdition if he doesn't change his ways. Then three other spirits or ghosts visit Scrooge: the ghost of Christmas past, the one of Christmas present; and the spirit of Christmas future. Each in turn shows Scrooge, in turn, who he was in his youth, who he is in the present, and what will happen to him in the future if he doesn't repent and turn from his greed and selfishness to embrace, instead, love, generosity, and compassion. If you haven't read the book—it's short—or seen one of the many versions of the movie or the play, do so.

There are multiple levels of meaning to Dickens's *A Christmas Carol*. It was written at the height of the industrial revolution in England. Unbridled capitalism had warped English life into the few who accumulated and controlled growing amounts of wealth and power, and millions—children included—committed by the system to the squalor and poverty of the industrial working class. Dickens wrote in another of his novels, *A Tale of Two Cities*, a line that captured the spirit of the age, "It was the best of times, it was the worst of times" (and so mirroring Ecclesiastes), but clearly the moral of *A Christmas Carol* was that greed and the acquisition of money led inevitably to the pit of hell, from where, as Jacob Marley sorrowfully told Scrooge, there was no escape, like the rich man in the tale of Lazarus. It reminds one of Paul's letters to his young friend Timothy: "Command those who are rich in this present world not to be arrogant nor to put their hope in wealth, which is so uncertain, but to put their hope in God, who richly provides us with everything for our enjoyment. Command them to do good, to be rich in good deeds, and to be generous and willing to share. In this way they will lay up treasure for themselves as a firm foundation for the coming age, so that they may take hold of the life that is truly life" (1 Tim 6:17–19).

That is as good verse to keep in mind as any other in Scripture as we consider the question inherent in the title to this chapter—what is valuable? You may even want to commit what it says to memory. While I'm not particularly good at memorizing Scriptures word for word, I do remember principles, especially those that contain a clear expression of God's will. Do not put your hope in wealth, but put instead hope and trust in God. God will provide for everything. That doesn't mean just "some" things, or "most" things, but just what it says, "everything." Be generous and share. This is the way of true life within the will of God.

Finally, before we leave Dickens and the *Christmas Carol*, let's filter it to distill the central truth: *real* wealth in this world has nothing to do with riches and money. It has all to do with caring, friendship, compassion, love, family, and sharing. It is remarkable how long-lived *A Christmas Carol* has been in our culture. Its meaning is just as important for us today—perhaps even more so—than when it was first published or performed in the middle of the nineteenth century.

During the Christmas service at a church in 2012, the music ministry and cast performed a wonderful show, devoted to—guess what?— how a man was so absorbed by his work that he forgot his family. He was "stressed" in modern parlance, perhaps "alienated" in more psychological terms, but the argument of the play was crystal clear: he had forgotten the family that looked to him for love and direction and affirmation. He had devoted himself to his work, thinking if he had just more and more of the material things, the rest would take care of itself. He felt he was working hard to get his children the latest electronic toys and that this would make them happy, when all they really wanted was his presence. If there was a dry eye in the audience that morning, there must have been some hearts of stone among us. For at the end, God and his messengers (the old spirits of Christmas present and Christmas future from the *Christmas Carol* updated a bit) melted the man's heart, he repented, and joyfully rejoined the human race as a full-fledged member, not as a solitary atom on his own quest for fortune and happiness.

And, while I was first composing this chapter, the awful massacre of the first graders in Newtown, Connecticut ripped through the heart and soul of this country. Everyone from the President on down was shocked and horrified at the cold-blooded killer, a twenty-year-old man so obviously alienated and alone, so awfully controlled by Satan to do his bidding. It may have had nothing directly to do with "what is valuable?" or "what is important?" but it does, in a larger fashion, demonstrate that an engrossment with self and one's interior monologues and even demonic voices and spirits, totally estranges you from God's will. So does accumulating wealth for its own sake, a subject we examine in the next chapter.

Questions for Discussion:

Okay, we have to take an honest pill before discussing some of these questions:

- Which is more valuable: wealth or wisdom?
- How much time do you spend each day reading or studying Scripture?
- How much time do you spend each day. Guess on percentages.
  - Watching television?
  - Talking or texting?
  - On the computer (aside from work-related matters; YouTube, for example, does *not* qualify as work)?
  - Playing a sport?
  - Watching the stock ticker tape?

- Is some kind of Bible software on your favorites or bookmarks list on your computer, or cell phone, or iPad, or any electronic peripheral?

- So, now, based on percentages of time spent doing one or all of the above, what is most valuable to you?

- Discuss the story of Lazarus (especially if you reading this as a Sunday school assignment with others).

4

Name It and Claim It

PERHAPS NO PHENOMENON OR trend in the modern Christian church has caused so much controversy as the "Name It and Claim It" or "prosperity" theology. Very roughly, it is invoked by those who believe passionately that one has but to ask God for something and God will provide. The keys are faith and standing on Scripture. And at the center of this theology is wealth. So let's examine it in a bit of revealing detail, not denying or confirming it, but explaining how wealth continues to be a contentious issue in a Christian's faith.

It is, as one should quickly note, not that simple! It was born in the modern Word of Faith churches—many of them Pentecostal, charismatic, and/ or non-denominational churches—sometimes described as Word churches because of a heavy reliance on the Word of God, or Scripture, for many of their beliefs and practices. That particular perspective—calling on Scripture to deny or support a particular belief system or theology—is of course not novel within the history of Christianity. It, after all, underlay the Protestant Reformation kicked off by Martin Luther when he posted his Ninety Five Theses on the doors of the church of Wittenberg in 1517. Luther's call for reform was essentially a call to cleanse the Church (the Roman Catholic Church) of all the accretions, rules, and regulations accrued since the time of the apostles. These are collectively sometimes referred to as Canon Law. Many of these were not scripturally based, such as the sale of indulgences, the celibacy of the priesthood, and the concept of purgatory, to name but a few. And Luther called for "Scripture Alone" as the rule for Christians.

The "Name it and Claim it" theologians of the late twentieth century laid the foundations of their relationship to God on several passages, including Matthew 7:7–11 and 1 John 5 14–15: "Ask and it will be given to you; seek and you will find; knock and the door will be opened to you. For everyone who asks receives; the one who seeks finds; and to the one who knocks, the door will be opened. Which of you, if your son asks for bread, will give him a stone? Or if he asks for a fish, will give him a snake? If you, then, though you are evil, know how to give good gifts to your children, how much more will your Father in heaven give good gifts to those who ask him!" (Matt 7:7–11). "This is the confidence we have in approaching God: that if we ask anything according to his will, he hears us. And if we know that he hears us—whatever we ask—we know that we have what we asked of him" (1 John 5:14–15).

These seem to suggest that one has but to ask God for wealth (described as prosperity in many instances), health, or anything else. The key to opening the cornucopia of God's kingdom was, or is, as the case may be, faith. One needs to have faith in the will of God to deliver on what he promises. One has to pray specifically for wealth, or health, or delivery, or whatever one is petitioning God for, and then "claim" it. Believers in this theology stand on Mark 11:22–24, "'Have faith in God,' Jesus answered. 'Truly I tell you, if anyone says to this mountain, "Go, throw yourself into the sea," and does not doubt in their heart but believes that what they say will happen, it will be done for them. Therefore I tell you, whatever you ask for in prayer, believe that you have received it, and it will be yours'" (Mark 11:22–24).

Many of these believers are organized and express their beliefs in churches called "word" churches, or "faith" churches, for obvious reasons, since they are standing on the word of God through faith. Sometimes they are called "word of faith" churches, which is drawn from Romans 10:8: "But what saith it? The word is nigh thee, even in thy mouth, and in thy heart: that is, the word of faith, which we preach" (King James Version).

Let's examine the movement a bit more carefully in this chapter, since wealth, and its creation and the desire for, is at the core of this small book examining wealth and work in the Bible. You will explore the historical evolution of work and especially of wealth in chapter 6 below, "How Work Got to be a Dirty Word."

While the modern prosperity message, and its followers and propagators, arose in the mid-twentieth century, wealth and its character and desirability, or, conversely, non-desirability, goes back deeply into the history of our country, to the time of the founders, to the era of the Puritans. Christians have in fact almost always struggled with wealth and how to approach this state of being, for lack of anything else to call it at the moment, just as the ancient Hebrews also approached the subject, sometimes gingerly, sometimes indirectly, sometimes like a clarion call, a loud Ram's horn blast, in the night.

Before getting to the Puritans, it is worthwhile noting that the earliest Christians, from the first century to the time of the Emperor Constantine (early fourth century) had few problems with wealth and its concomitant ally, power. The earliest churches were generally humble affairs, as were the earliest Christians, although from its beginnings Christianity attracted people from all walks of life. But its powerful message of redemption and forgiveness, of certainty in an uncertain world, of the promise of a future eternity in God's heaven, of humility and service, and of a powerful morality whose core was deliverance from the problems of today's world and a certainty in the next, struck a powerful chord with the poor and disenfranchised within the Roman Empire.

The Christians as outsiders gradually changed over the course of the three centuries from age of the death and resurrection of Jesus in the first century to the age of the Emperor Constantine. As the sect grew, so did its ability to attract more than Jews (the proverbial outsiders in the Roman Empire because of their dogged insistence on the singularity of their religion) and the poor. Its message resonated with all classes, even from as early as the travels and teachings of the Apostle Paul in the first century, and gradually drew in people from all walks of life, including soldiers, philosophers and intellectuals, merchants, and finally, with the coming of Constantine, they even converted the Emperor himself.

In AD 313 (or CE, or common or Christian era if you prefer) he allowed for religious toleration across the empire with the Edict of Milan, ending the persecution of Christians, and in 324 he took one crucial step further: he made Christianity the *official* religion of Rome and her empire.

Constantine is a complex character and debate still flows around him and about what he did, but that does not concern us right now. What does concern us is that he opened the door to power and wealth for Christianity, although of course there already were plenty of Christians around who had reached high levels of achievement, wealth, and some power in the empire. Constantine's mother was one such individual who became a devout follower of Jesus, and early on pressed on her son the message of Christianity. Mothers do have a way with sons!

But, until Constantine, there was always the threat that some emperor would turn on the Christians officially and persecute them. After Constantine, although one or two emperors attempted to restore the old pagan worship to equality with the new official religion, Christianity became associated with the power and wealth of the Roman Empire, which, ironically was about to enter a gradual era of decline. But it only "fell" slowly (as in the rise and "fall" of the Roman Empire) over the centuries, and the Christian faith was eventually transmitted to the successors of the Roman Empire—barbarian invaders from across northern Europe and the steppes of Asia for example—and a new era was kicked off by Constantine and those who came after him.

The Papacy grew in influence and power, and wealth, and the Church became the quintessential symbol of security and continuity. It also became rich during the Middle Ages, even with all the obvious and not-so-obvious exceptions, such as the powerful monastic movement that stressed, at least in its avowed principles, obedience, celibacy, and, interestingly enough, *poverty*, which we may take for this little book as meaning the pretty exact opposite of *wealth*.

Monasticism started in the deserts of Syria and Egypt as early as the first century when solitary Christians, called hermits, occasionally took to the empty and hard-scrabble deserts of the land to "get away from it all" and get closer to God. The hermits eventually banded together for protection in small groups to further their similar agendas and the word "monk" was applied to those embracing this life.[1] By the fourth and fifth centuries, certain members of the clergy, St. Augustine of Hippo and St. Benedict of Nursia, for example, wrote up rules for governing monks living together as monks and friars. These are two different names for men who banded together for basically the same ends, with the primary distinction being that friars were evangelists and preachers as well as monks. They didn't simply retire to a monastery, but their vocation took them beyond the walls of the monastery to preach, teach, and evangelize. These followers of Augustine, or of Benedict, or later of Saint Dominic or Saint Francis, became known by the rules or order established by their founders, thus we have Benedictines, Augustinians, Franciscans, Dominicans, etc., all monastic orders with different

---

1. Within the Christian Church: such a person typically lived a celibate life according to the rule of a particular order . . . and adhered to vows, esp. of poverty, chastity, and obedience. In England, the term was not applied before the Reformation to members of the mendicant orders, who were always called *friars*. Since then, however, it has been widely used of the members of these orders. In French and German the equivalent of *monk* is applied equally to 'monks' and 'friars'" ("monk" in the Oxford English Dictionary, The Definitive Record of the English Language. " monk, n.1". OED Online. December 2014. Oxford University Press. http://www.oed.com/view/Entry/121259?result=1&rskey=V5gZnr& (accessed December 15, 2014).

sets of rules, but *all* still ruled by the three basic principles of obedience (to the order), celibacy, and poverty.

Why the emphasis on poverty we should ask? Did not the Old Testament equate poverty with the absence of God's blessings in one's life? See chapter 7, "Some Very Hard Truths," for more details on what the Scripture said about wealth, and its concomitant, the absence of wealth or poverty. Why were saints such as Francis of Assisi (1181–1226) so devoted to poverty and actually *sought* it with all their devotion and will?

Francis left the good life into which he was born, renounced his heritage and worldly possessions, and took to begging to keep him alive as he preached and taught the message of Jesus which Francis sought to live out literally. Francis's devotion constituted a remarkable repudiation of worldly values, and a concomitant substitution for those that Jesus taught. Four verses from the book of Matthew, chapter 6, well summarize the theology of a Francis of Assisi whose insistence on absolute poverty was thought by many to be bordering on the insane: "Do not store up for yourselves treasures on earth, where moths and vermin destroy, and where thieves break in and steal. But store up for yourselves treasures in heaven, where moths and vermin do not destroy, and where thieves do not break in and steal. For where your treasure is, there your heart will be also . . . No one can serve two masters. Either you will hate the one and love the other, or you will be devoted to the one and despise the other. You cannot serve both God and money" (Matt 6:19–21, 24).

Those are pretty plain and clear admonitions. They eschew worldly values—such as that wealth and prosperity are good—and embrace values that do not seem, at least on the surface, very realistic given the world we inhabit. Francis was a radical believer in absolute poverty. He wouldn't even let his followers have a psalter (a copy of the Book of Psalms) for fear that one friar would have a bigger one than another, perhaps one more beautifully embellished, and thus open the door to discord and envy.

When Francis died, he already had a following organized into an order recognized by the Pope, and they soon divided over those devoted to the purity of Francis's calling and those who recognized that some accommodations needed to be made with the "world" to further God's programs here on earth. The Franciscans grew into one of the most powerful orders in the Church, always looking for that delicate balance between the principles so nobly taken up by Francis and the need to live in a "fallen" world, governed by the human concerns with wealth, power, sex, pride, and hubris, many of these sins so well described in Proverbs 6:16–19.

Other passages from the New Testaments support Francis and his general view of wealth. "Keep your lives free from the lust for money: be content with what you have. God has said: 'I will never leave you nor forsake you,'" Paul wrote to the Hebrews, adding, "we, therefore, can confidently say: 'The Lord is my helper; I will not fear. What can man do to me?'"

And in his letter to the Ephesians, Paul stated the case just as emphatically, calling the love of money for what it was: greed. "But among you there must not be even a hint of sexual immorality, or of any kind of impurity, or of greed, because these are improper for God's holy people"[2]

In Luke Jesus spells it out clearly also, on the meaning of wealth. "Someone in the crowd said to him, 'Teacher, tell my brother to divide the inheritance with me.' Jesus replied, 'Man, who appointed me a judge or an arbiter between you?' Then he said to them, 'Watch out! Be on your guard against all kinds of greed; life does not consist in an abundance of possessions.'"[3] That's as clear as Jesus could make it, unequivocal and declarative. Life does not consist in acquiring and having possessions.

And then Jesus followed up, just to be sure he was understood perfectly.

> And he told them this parable: "The ground of a certain rich man yielded an abundant harvest. He thought to himself, 'What shall I do? I have no place to store my crops.'
>
> "Then he said, 'This is what I'll do. I will tear down my barns and build bigger ones, and there I will store my surplus grain.' And I'll say to myself, 'You have plenty of grain laid up for many years. Take life easy; eat, drink and be merry.'
>
> "But God said to him, 'You fool! This very night your life will be demanded from you. Then who will get what you have prepared for yourself?'
>
> "This is how it will be with whoever stores up things for themselves but is not rich toward God."[4]

And one other instruction from Jesus, which probably rang with warm and tender familiarity among those that St. Francis called upon to lead his life. "Then he called the crowd to him along with his disciples and

2. Eph 5:3, NIV.

3. Luke 12:13.

4. Luke 12:16–21.

said: 'Whoever wants to be my disciple must deny themselves and take up their cross and follow me. For whoever wants to save their life will lose it, but whoever loses their life for me and for the gospel will save it. What good is it for someone to gain the whole world, yet forfeit their soul? Or what can anyone give in exchange for their soul?'"[5]

The ageless problem of dealing with wealth did not abate with the coming of the Reformation in the sixteenth century. Although Protestants hurled quite a bit of invective and heaped accusations on the Church for its wealth—manifested in many ways by the life and nature of Popes, benefices, great cathedrals, control of land and resources, etc.—and how that wealth and its manipulation undermined the Church's true vocation, Protestants were soon at odds with the same issues. It was in these times that the Puritans emerged, first in England but one can recognize their essential doctrine across the face of rising Protestantism. The great dilemma of Puritans was how to reconcile prosperity (or another face of wealth) with a godly life. The stage that this played out most vividly was set in the "wilderness" of the New World, especially along the English colonies stretched out like a thin line of "civilization" on the east coast of North America from New England to Georgia.

Nobody caught the Puritan dilemma better than the distinguished historian Edmund S. Morgan in his classic study *The Puritan Dilemma: The Story of John Winthrop* first published in 1958, with many subsequent editions.

> Puritanism required that man refrain from sin, but told him he would sin anyhow. Puritanism required that he reform the world in the image of God's holy kingdom but taught him that the evil of the world was incurable and inevitable. Puritanism required that he work to the best of his ability at whatever task was set before him and partake of the good things that god had filled the world with but told him he must enjoy his work and his pleasures only, as it were, absent-mindedly, with attention fixed on God.[6]

That's a curious phrase to use, "absent-mindedly," as if the Puritans could see a ghost in the night, but simply chose to ignore it and go into the dark woods of pleasure and wealth, whistling to keep their spirits up and, hopefully, keep the wolves at bay.

This was only the first half of the Puritan dilemma: what to do with the wealth I was accumulating by my hard work and determination. Or,

5. Mark 8:34–38.
6. Morgan, *The Puritan Dilemma*, 8.

again as Morgan phrased it, the central Puritan dilemma was "the problem of doing right in a world that does wrong."[7] As the Puritans accumulated more wealth, they had to deal with it. They were part of "the world," or in the world, but were enjoined in several scriptural passages *not* to be a part of it.[8] How is a man supposed to be in the world but not of the world? That question plagued the Puritans and continues to dog us today. They seem like irreconcilable ends.

In this instance, and it runs like a thread through American history, wealth is a reward for a godly life devoted to work, devotion, faith, and good behavior, but it brings with it the concomitant evil of distancing us from God by attributing our good fortunes to ourselves.

The Protestant work ethic—celebrated and given a clear modern identity by Max Weber in the early twentieth century—was also emerging and we'll deal with that aspect of Scripture, what it says about work, fully in the next chapter.

The second half of the Puritan dilemma was that the Puritan—being a good Calvinist—was never altogether certain if he was truly saved. As Morgan so felicitously phrased it, "these paradoxical, not to say contradictory, requirements affected different people in different ways. Some lived in agony of uncertainty, wondering each day whether God had singled them out for eternal glory or eternal torment."[9] This, of course, was a summary of

---

7. Morgan, *Puritan Dilemma*, 203.

8. "If you were of the world, the world would love its own. Yet because you are not of the world, but I chose you out of the world, therefore the world hates you" (John 15:19).

"I have given them Your word; and the world has hated them because they are not of the world, just as I am not of the world. I do not pray that You should take them out of the world, but that You should keep them from the evil one. They are not of the world, just as I am not of the world" (John 17:14).

"Pure and undefiled religion before God and the Father is this: to visit orphans and widows in their trouble, and to keep oneself unspotted from the world" (Jas 1:27).

"Do not love the world or the things in the world. If anyone loves the world, the love of the Father is not in him. For all that is in the world—the lust of the flesh, the lust of the eyes, and the pride of life—is not of the Father but is of the world. And the world is passing away, and the lust of it; but he who does the will of God abides forever" (1 John 2:15).

"Adulterers and adulteresses! Do you not know that friendship with the world is enmity with God? Whoever therefore wants to be a friend of the world makes himself an enemy of God" (Jas 4:4).

The above passages quote from the website: http://www.bible-knowledge.com/in-world-not-of-it/.

9. Morgan, *Puritan Dilemma*, 11.

the doctrine of predestination. That doctrine is based on several scriptural passages identified in this footnote.[10]

In its simplest form, God chose certain people to be saved for all eternity. And those not chosen went, of course, the other way, to eternal perdition. At stake here was nothing less than your life forever after death on earth, and the Puritans took this very, very seriously, as many, of course, still do today.

Two great biblical principles seemingly contradict each other in this scenario: one, God's omnipotence and sovereignty, and thus his ability to predestine people according to his will; and two, man's free will, also ordained by God. Both are supported by multiple scriptures. Let's examine this issue a bit since wealth became for many Puritans a source of comfort, assuming that God had blessed them, and the blessings of wealth and comfort itself were thought by some to be testimony to being among the elect, or predestined to eternal salvation. On the other hand, to be among the poor was somehow to be associated with sin and being out of God's favor. That too is supported by Scripture. We examine that in chapter 7, "Some Very Hard Truths."

On predestination, one of the principal passages is Romans 8:29–30, where Paul writes to the church at Rome, "For those God foreknew he also *predestined* [italics added] to be conformed to the image of his Son, that he might be the firstborn among many brothers and sisters. And those he *predestined* [italics added], he also called; those he called, he also justified; those he justified, he also glorified."

---

10. Acts 13:48: "And when the Gentiles heard this, they began rejoicing and glorifying the word of the Lord; and as many as had been appointed to eternal life believed."

John 1:12–13: "But as many as received Him, to them He gave the right to become children of God, even to those who believe in His name, who were born not of blood, nor of the will of the flesh, nor the will of man, but of God."

Philippians 1:29: "For to you it has been granted for Christ's sake, not only to believe in Him, but also suffer for his sake."

Romans 8:29–30: "For whom He foreknew, He also predestined to become conformed to the image of His Son, that He might be the first-born among many brethren; and whom He predestined, these He also called; and whom He called, these He also justified; and whom He justified, these He also glorified."

Ephesians 1:5: "He predestined us to adoption as sons through Jesus Christ to Himself, according to the kind intention of His will."

Ephesians 1:11: "Also we have obtained and inheritance, having been predestined according to His purpose who works all things after the counsel of His will."

From a website called The Calvinist Corner, http://www.calvinistcorner.com/predestination.htm.

Furthermore, in Ephesians, Paul writes: "Praise be to the God and Father of our Lord Jesus Christ, who has blessed us in the heavenly realms with every spiritual blessing in Christ. For he chose us in him before the creation of the world to be holy and blameless in his sight. In love he *predestined* [italics added] us for adoption to sonship through Jesus Christ, in accordance with his pleasure and will—to the praise of his glorious grace, which he has freely given us in the One he loves."[11]

Other Scriptures are equally forceful, both in the New and the Old Testaments. "For many are called, but few [are] chosen."[12] And, "before I formed you in the womb I knew you, before you were born I set you apart; I appointed you as a prophet to the nations."[13]

We won't belabor the point that God is indeed a sovereign God who has acted to select some and not others. Or, for the context of this book, some are chosen to be wealthy and others not. I know this line will fly in the face of those of you reading, and thinking, "but *I* am responsible for my destiny and *I* made this wealth," but Scripture is quite clear on predestination: God made you and predestined you for wealth, or, conversely, poverty. Let's not worry about the middle ground for the moment. You'll get that in the chapter on the Protestant work ethic.

In seeming contradiction to the doctrine of predestination stands the doctrine or principle of free will, or, you have the right to choose which path to take in your life. Scripture is very clear on this as well, and theologians and serious laymen have argued over which is correct for two thousand years. It was a major point of contention that led to the Protestant Reformation of the sixteenth century and even divided the great leaders, like Martin Luther and Erasmus of Rotterdam, of that reform movement. So which is it? Are we predestined by a sovereign God for salvation or to damnation, for wealth or poverty, or do we have free will to determine what to do with our lives, and thus, consequently, to craft our lives? The answer is both complex and simple. We are both predestined *and* we have free will.

In this chapter on "Name It and Claim It" we are ranging a bit, but it is important to establish the scriptural credentials of the free will doctrine, since it underlays one of the bases by which we acquire wealth, and that road to wealth involves work. Prefiguring chapter 5 on work a bit, Edmund Morgan in his book on the Puritans clearly explained their attitude towards work.

11. Eph 1:3–6.
12. Matt 22:14, KJV.
13. Jer 1:5, NIV.

By the age of thirty, John Winthrop had established in his own mind that work could lead to pleasure, and, indeed, work itself was a form of pleasure that God had provided for him. "He had learned to stick to business. If he worked hard at whatever task lay before him, he could take his pleasures in stride."

"Of course," Morgan continued, "work itself could be a snare," as so many workaholics have discovered over the years. "It was easy to become engrossed in it for its own sake or for the sake of the worldly rewards it brought. A man who labored merely for gain, with no thought for God, was no better than a libertine."[14] Work could be an end in itself.

"But he who worked because God willed it, multiplying his talents like a good and faithful servant, could throw himself into his job almost as a way of worship, without fear of losing balance," observed Morgan, invoking the parable of the faithful servant. "That he might amass a fortune in the process was an incidental benefit, not to be treated as a goal, but not to be rejected if it came."[15]

Remember the title to this chapter, "Name It and Claim It." Keep your eyes focused on wealth since that is what this is all about.

In numerous websites, and that may well be an understatement, wealth and riches are the principal themes. One claims that there are more than 800 scriptures "about money," and I don't doubt it.[16] There may be more scripture about wealth and money, in fact, than any other subject in the Bible. Some are practical, devoted to what Scripture has to say about budgeting, debt, family, saving, and career, while others, such as "The Bible and Money: 10 Tips from Scripture," at Beliefnet.com are useful reminders of where wealth comes from and how to handle it.[17]

As we examine wealth, some of these tips are very useful as we consider the "name it and claim it" philosophy.

---

14. Morgan, *Puritan Dilemma*, 14.

15. Ibid. The parable of the faithful servant appears in one form or another in all four gospels, the longest in Matthew 25:14–30. Interestingly, some translations call it the parable of the talents, others the parable of the gold bags, others the parable of the faithful servants.

16. See Dave Ramsey's Financial Peace University: http://www.daveramsey.com/church/scriptures/.

17. http://www.beliefnet.com/Faiths/Christianity/2008/09/The-Bible-and-Money-10-Tips-from-Scripture.aspx?p=3.

As I always say to someone who wants to write a book but doesn't know where to begin: "Try with the first sentence." In that spirit, here are the ten tips.

From Deuteronomy comes the first: Remember that God creates wealth. "Remember the Lord your God, for it is He who gives the ability to produce wealth."[18]

Number 2 is labeled "Feeling rich? Give thanks to God, and quotes from Jeremiah 9:23-24. "This is what the Lord says: 'Let not the wise man boast of his wisdom or the strong man boast of his strength or the rich man boast of his riches, but let him who boats boast about this: that he understands and knows Me, that I am the Lord, who exercises kindness, justice and righteousness on earth, for in these I delight,' declares the Lord."

From Proverbs 13:22, "A good man leaves an inheritance to his children's children," summarized as "Save for the kids' inheritance."

Debt tip number 4 is "Get out of debt in order to be free," drawn from Proverbs 22:7: "The poor are always ruled over by the rich, so don't borrow and put yourself under their power." As I type that I remember all the loans that have made my life comfortable and possible, from the house mortgage to the car loans. And, what if I wanted to be entrepreneurial and start a small business with a small business loan? My point is that we sometimes need to interpret Scripture in the light of the culture when it was written, and our culture today.

"Guard against greed," is tip number 5, which draws from Luke 12:15. "Then [Jesus] said to them, 'Watch out! Be on your guard against all kinds of greed; a man's life does not consist in the abundance of his possessions.'"

One of my favorite verses, often misquoted, was written by the Apostle Paul to his young disciple Timothy. "For the love of money is the root of all sorts of evil, and some people by longing for it have wandered away from the faith and pierced themselves with many griefs."[19] The tip, number 6, that they draw from that is obvious, but well worth recalling. "Remember that money isn't evil, but loving it is."

Tip number 7, "Give back to God," recalls tip 1: God is the one who produces all wealth. Number 7 draws upon Proverbs 3:9, "Honor the Lord with your wealth, with the firstfruits of all your crops; then your barns will be filled to overflowing, and your vats will brim over with new wine," Or,

18. Deut 8:18.
19. 1 Tim 6:10.

as my wife Louise is prone to remind me occasionally: "You can't out give God. He will always return more than you give."

"Know that everything belongs to God," is tip number 8, drawing from Leviticus 25:23. "And remember the land is Mine, so you may not sell it permanently. You are merely My tenants and sharecroppers." For those of you with strong feelings for the land or property you own, sometimes going back generations into the distant past, this is a hard lesson. We are sojourners here on earth. But if God puts them into your trust, you can enjoy the usufruct happily and joyfully, always remembering the source of your happiness. And remember, what was valid for an agricultural and pastoral culture 2500 or more years ago may have a different meaning and interpretation in a modern, industrial or post-industrial society such as the modern world.

Tip number 9 reminds us to "Put God before money," which seems quite obvious, but the obvious has to be restated, reread, and recommitted often to keep God's will and ways before us. Matthew 6:33 is quoted: "But seek first His kingdom and His righteousness, and all these things will be given to you as well."

And, finally, a very practical tip on how to handle your wealth and money, "Count the cost of your spending," which draws upon Luke 14:28, "For which of you, intending to build a tower, does not sit down first and count the cost, whether he has enough to finish it." This also speaks to being a good steward of the resources and wealth that God has put in your hands.

Wealth occupies an immense proportion of the attention of Scripture precisely because it can cause so much woe, all the way from acquiring so much to having so little. Closely associated with wealth is work, for it is from work that wealth is derived, keeping always in mind that the hand of God is the true purveyor. At the core of the "Name it and Claim it" philosophy, in the most positive possible terms to interpret it, is to claim what God has provided for you by remembering his words and promises and standing on them through faith. In the worst possible interpretation, critics accuse "Name it and Claim it" theologians and preachers of treating God as a jukebox or vending machine—put a coin in, choose your song or your food or drink, and press the button, and God will deliver. That is not fair to those who truly believe in the promises of God.

Let's leave wealth aside for the moment, but never entirely, and focus in the next chapter on work, especially on the "work ethic" associated with one of the most significant expression of Christianity in the world, modern

Protestantism. A strong work ethic usually produces a bounty of wealth and therein lay some problems for Christians trying to deal, not with failure and defeat, but with wealth and success.

Questions for Discussion:

- In a nutshell, what is the "Name It and Claim It" theology/phenomenon?

- What role does Scripture and Faith play in "Name It and Claim It?"

- Why does wealth have such a powerful pull on us? [Big question category]

- What did Constantine do that so changed the nature of the church?

- Why monasticism?

- What was the Puritan dilemma? Or, more exactly, what were the Puritan dilemmas?

- Are any of them (the Puritan dilemmas) relevant in our world today?

- How do predestination and free will apparently contradict each other?

- Why is wealth such a difficult subject to deal with when we all want some?

5

Work and the Protestant Work Ethic

Go to the ant, you lazybones;
consider its ways, and be wise.[1]

PERHAPS THE CENTRAL QUESTION on this aspect of life is: is work a means
or an end? Or, framed another way, *why* do we work?

Scripture holds everyone accountable for not only "good works," but
also for work itself as a godly way of life.[2]

The lessons, instructions, and metaphors are sometimes pure poetry—
not an easy achievement when dealing with the humdrum subject of work.

Go to the ant, you sluggard;
consider its ways and be wise!
It has no commander,
no overseer or ruler,
yet it stores its provisions in summer
and gathers its food at harvest.
How long will you lie there, you sluggard?
When will you get up from your sleep?
A little sleep, a little slumber,
a little folding of the hands to rest—
and poverty will come on you like a thief
and scarcity like an armed man.[3]

1. Prov 6:6.

2. Close students of the rise of Protestantism, and of books like the book of James,
will instantly recognize that there is dimension of the relationship between faith and
works that is not mentioned in this narrative. We have simply elected to keep the focus
on wealth and work very tightly in this small book.

3. Prov 6:6–11.

The Apostle Paul made it perfectly clear why we work, leaving the poetic form for the inspired writers of the Old Testament. Paul sometimes got straight to the point: "For even when we were with you, we gave you this rule: 'The one who is unwilling to work shall not eat'" (2 Thess 3:10).

But even the poets were clear on the relationship between work and poverty, although couching the message—typically—in a slightly more metaphorical form: "Do not love sleep or you will grow poor; stay awake and you will have food to spare" (Prov 20:13).

From Ecclesiastes comes the following comfort food for those who love to toil and work and accumulate.

> This is what I have observed to be good: that it is appropriate for a person to eat, to drink and to find satisfaction in their toilsome labor under the sun during the few days of life God has given them—for this is their lot. Moreover, when God gives someone wealth and possessions, and the ability to enjoy them, to accept their lot and be happy in their toil—this is a gift of God. They seldom reflect on the days of their life, because God keeps them occupied with gladness of heart (Eccl 5:18–20).

Paul wrote the Thessalonians in a kind of irritated fashion about working and idleness. And he was very explicit about naming his example of working as a model for all to follow. Note the last sentence in this brief passage. "The one who is unwilling to work shall not eat."

> In the name of the Lord Jesus Christ, we command you, brothers and sisters, to keep away from every believer who is idle and disruptive and does not live according to the teaching you received from us. For you yourselves know how you ought to follow our example. We were not idle when we were with you, nor did we eat anyone's food without paying for it . . . we worked night and day, laboring and toiling so that we would not be a burden to any of you. We did this, not because we do not have the right to such help, but in order to offer ourselves as a model for you to imitate. For even when we were with you, we gave you this rule: "The one who is unwilling to work shall not eat.[4]

In the Old Testament, in the book of Deuteronomy in a long passage on our obligations to the poor and the needy, the writer, usually thought to be Moses, addresses directly how God will bless the hands of those who work. "Give generously to them [the poor] and do so without a grudging

4. 2 Thess 3:6–10.

heart; then because of this the Lord your God will bless you in all your work and in everything you put your hand to. There will always be poor people in the land. Therefore I command you to be openhanded toward your fellow Israelites who are poor and needy in your land."[5]

In a rather direct fashion, the blessings of work—especially of wealth accumulated—are then the substance we share with the poor, usually, of course, as tithes and offerings that pass through our hands to our churches and then out to the community, both local and global. The more we have, the more we can share.

Paul in his letter to Timothy is clear about this relationship between work and wealth and sharing it. "Command those who are rich in this present world not to be arrogant nor to put their hope in wealth, which is so uncertain, but to put their hope in God, who richly provides us with everything for our enjoyment. Command them to do good, to be rich in good deeds, and to be generous and willing to share. In this way they will lay up treasure for themselves as a firm foundation for the coming age, so that they may take hold of the life that is truly life."[6]

In our own history, the greatest of the Protestants of colonial America, the Puritans, struggled with some theological issues arising from the themes of wealth and work.

Briefly, the Puritans thoroughly believed in predestination, or the teaching that some men (and we'll not be politically correct and gender sensitive in this book, especially when dealing with Puritans) were selected, or elected, by God for salvation, and, by definition, some weren't (double predestination).

Since no one could know exactly if he was saved, the Puritans worked fast and furious in colonial America, largely New England, to demonstrate or prove somehow that they were among the elect.

It was thought one of the principal ways one could recognize one was blessed by God and among the chosen was if one had good fortune and accumulated wealth. So, working hard and accumulating wealth (which, of course, was one of the contributing streams to capitalism) became a cornerstone of American life.

The scriptural bases for predestination are in the following verses:

> In love he predestined us for adoption to sonship through Jesus
> Christ, in accordance with his pleasure and will—to the praise of

5. Deut 15:10–11.

6. 1 Tim 6:17–19.

his glorious grace, which he has freely given us in the One he loves (parts of Eph 4, 5, 6).

For those God foreknew he also predestined to be conformed to the image of his Son, that he might be the firstborn among many brothers and sisters. And those he predestined, he also called; those he called, he also justified; those he justified, he also glorified (Rom 8:29–30).

We'll not follow John Calvin's logic, expressed largely in his *Institutes of the Christian Religion*, but simply remark that the "Protestant work ethic" that arose to explain the nexus between the Puritans and work and their faith remained strong in American history.

Max Weber's *The Protestant Ethic and the Spirit of Capitalism* describes the relationship between the ethics of Protestantism and the emergence of the spirit of modern capitalism.[7] Written and revised in various forms in the late nineteenth and early twentieth centuries, Weber addressed one of the great challenges of modern civilization: how did so much wealth come into being, and at the heart of his findings is the claim that "religious forces, not simply economic ones, paved the way for the mentality characteristic of modern, Western capitalism."[8]

Or, put slightly another way, "our secular and materialistic culture is partly indebted to a *spiritual* revolution: the Protestant Reformation of the sixteenth century." And, as his editors and translators noted, "that Weber's argument raises—or begs—a hundred questions is inseparable from its eminence and renown."[9]

We need not get bogged down in the various forms or expressions of Christianity that encouraged capitalism. Suffice it to mention that the Protestant variety that developed especially in England and the United States, and among certain portions of European nations such as Germany, in contrast to traditional Catholicism, stressed or developed attributes such as "free institutions, effective parliaments, and responsible and dynamic leaders," all mentalities and political advantages that favored "business acumen and professional advancement."[10]

---

7 Weber, *The Protestant Ethic*. I profited from a useful summary in SparkNotes, known by generations of undergraduate students as a quick source of much useful information: http://www.sparknotes.com/philosophy/protestantethic/context.html.

8. Weber, *The Protestant Ethic*, ix.

9. Ibid.

10. Ibid., x–xi.

Weber broke with a number of prior givens or conceptions within Western civilization that were considered "historically novel, radical, and momentous," most specifically with pre-capitalist attitudes towards work. Weber suggested that civilizations prior to the rise of capitalism, or say roughly those before the sixteenth century, "tend to see it [work] as a necessary evil, to be expedited solely in order to live and as part of the never-ending, meaningless cycle of production and consumption."[11] Remember, Weber, often thought as the founder of modern sociology, was also an economist who viewed man, in the pre-capitalist era, as merely a laborer working to meet his economic needs. Once these were satisfied—food, shelter and a little spending money—and "since work has no intrinsic value," both worker and employer ceased to strive to move faster or more efficiently for any given economic end. In other words, one's work was simply a means to an end, and since those ends over the centuries leading up to capitalism did not change much, neither did productivity or attitudes towards work.

"In contrast to these traditional attitudes," Weber's editors wrote, "consider next the mental and moral universe of early capitalist entrepreneurs, as Weber describes it. No longer is work deemed a meaningless chore to be finished as soon as possible. Now it is invested with moral value. For employers imbued with this new 'spirit,' economic activity is an end in itself, central to their identity, a calling with rigorous implications that transgress old ways of doing business."[12] And "Weber's own characterization of the 'spirit' of capitalism, which he illustrated copiously with quotations from Benjamin Franklin, sought to reconstruct attitudes and motivations toward work that he believed were uniquely modern." And then, assuming all of the above is true, the key question was "but where had they come from?"[13]

By now, if you have been reading this book, you should be asking yourself, "Helloooooooo, what about the Bible, Max? Therein one can find many mandates, rules, admonishments, and wisdom about work, and it is *not* just a means to an end, but a vocation in itself." But before nailing Weber for failing to take Scripture into account in his analysis, let's continue with the question, "where had they [the new attitudes and motivations toward work] come from" and his answer.

Even Weber's admirers admit he is a bit fuzzy on this question, "his answer was more evasive than he was willing to admit."

11. Weber, *The Protestant Ethic*, xvi.
12. Ibid., xvii.
13. Ibid.

"But the general thrust of his argument," they write, "is that the *ethos* of modern capitalism—that is, its distinctive moral attitudes toward economic activity and work, its methodical, specialized style of life—is historically indebted (caused by, congruent with) the Protestant *ethic*: the ascetic movement that arose out of the Protestant Reformation and its aftermath."[14]

"Work gained an unprecedented dignity by being understood as a vocation or calling (*Beruf*) ordained by God." Now we're getting warmer to, in fact, what the Bible says, which Weber, as a very rational economist, was probably not very familiar with. The Bible states the link between work and vocation and the will of God very clearly. Weber's editors don't. "The link between Protestant ethic and capitalist ethos (spirit) is one of the most complex aspects of Weber's essay."[15]

The problem is that Weber does not look far enough back into Christianity to see a clear exposition of the significance and meaning of work in Scripture, most of which appeared almost 2000 years before Weber, 1500 years before the rise of capitalism, and sometimes even 2500–3000 years before Weber's time. He is interested in how capitalism came into being, and so he focuses rather tightly on when "Protestantism" came into being largely in the sixteenth century.

"Among Weber's most famous claims," his editors note, "in *The Protestant Ethic* is the contention that Calvinism constituted the supercharged motivation behind the ascetic movement and its sectarian splinters."[16] Moving right along, the editors analyze Calvinism in Weber. "The Calvinist doctrine of predestination, according to which all humans are irrevocably either damned or chosen to be among God's elect, posed an agonizing question to the faithful."[17] True enough. "Were they the vessels of God's grace or simply worthless creatures condemned to the unending torment of hell?" This led to the next question which we dealt with in some substance in the chapter on the Puritans. How did one know one was saved, or, conversely, damned?

Stick with me here, for we are deepening this probe into work and its meaning, not only in Scripture, but in how modern society has chosen to interpret what work means to man and his society.

"God's will could not be manipulate or deciphered," Weber's editors claimed, following Weber. And here we move a bit closer to what Weber

14. Ibid., xvii-xviii.

15. Ibid, xviii.

16. Ibid.

17. Ibid.

was getting at. "But could intimations of his divine purpose for humans be revealed to the faithful?"[18]

As we know from studying the Puritans and John Winthrop, the answer could be yes, no, or maybe, not at all satisfying, but they *were* dealing with God's will in an area that was gray to the Puritan divines, that is to say the intersection between God's sovereignty and man's free will. Now we are slowly closing the circle, finding the answer Weber suggested as to how Calvinism led to a work ethic.

According to the editors and Weber, it was Puritan and Calvinist divines, in their answers to "are we saved?" who led the way. "They [Puritan ministers and theologians] were encouraged to assume that 'tireless labor in a calling was . . . the best possible means of attaining this self-assurance [that they were saved].'"[19] So there you have it. You work, accumulate, invest, invent, trade and build your house of work, and its success will be *prima facie* evidence of God's providential grace on you, and a witness to your salvation.

Weber's essay, first published in 1905 and with many subsequent editions, "was attacked as theoretically confused, imaginatively fanciful, and historically wrong . . . [and] the essay has been criticized for overestimating the importance of religious motives and of the Protestant petite bourgeoisie in the emergence of capitalism."[20] And Catholic pre-Reformation merchants and bankers were ignored as vehicles of capitalism, as were other historical signposts along the way.

What makes *The Protestant Ethic* so persistent and survivable was not its absolute veracity, but "because of its utility; its protean aptitude . . . to act as a catalyst of hypotheses or vehicle of multiple projects that have little to do with the impulse that originally animated it," as the editors noted.[21] Or, in plain English, it continues to stimulate thinking on work and its concomitant, wealth, across religions, across cultures, across all parts of the world. How, for example, does the Protestant work ethic apply to one of the most successful modern capitalist societies created in a part of the world, Japan, devoted to faith traditions removed from Christianity, like Buddhism, Shintoism, and Confucianism?

18. Ibid., xvii-xx.
19. Ibid., xvii–xix.
20. Ibid., xxii.
21. Ibid., xxix.

Returning to the Western world, "Weber's conclusion was that Calvinism promoted, despite itself, an emotional inducement in the faithful to look for 'proof' of 'election'; and that methodical, systematic work in a calling was the social product of this religious quest." Again, in plain English, the search for salvation resulted in working hard to prove it. That Scripture not only approved of work, as we have seen, but also encouraged work, labor, enterprise, whatever we want to label it, reinforced what the editors identified was a central theme in Weber's thinking, that "work . . . was the social product of this religious quest."[22] Remember, this was a pioneering work of sociology by Weber and so the terminology may be laborious and freighted with jargon, but what he was saying was that that the religious quest of the Calvinists—are we saved and if we suspect not, then how *do we* obtain the much desired salvation for all eternity?—drove them to look for proof, and they surmised that God-given prosperity and wealth, which would be the fruit of their labors, was a most visible evidence or testimony to their salvation.

Not all Puritans and Calvinists viewed this relationship as valid. Some, like an early member of the Massachusetts Bay Colony, argued with the Puritan divines about the relationship between work, and "works," or doing good things, and salvation.

In 1637 one of the most celebrated trials in early American history was held in Boston. At the end of it, Anne Hutchinson, a mother of fifteen children, was most unceremoniously booted out of the Massachusetts Bay Colony presided over by the Puritans building their "city upon a hill," or the New Jerusalem.

The Massachusetts Bay Colony, governed by John Winthrop, was made up largely of Puritans, a strain of Protestantism in England that was most avowedly and openly "puritanical" in its constitution and behavior. As such, it strikes us today as seething with intolerance, bigotry, and prejudice.

Anne Hutchinson was, on the other hand, a strong woman who knew her Bible and was not afraid of stating explicitly and with passion what it said, even if it contradicted the collected wisdom of the ministers in the colony. For doing this, she was excommunicated from the church and banished from the colony.

She crossed the Atlantic to the Massachusetts colony in 1634 with her husband, William, who was almost always overshadowed by his aggressive, some would say defiant, wife. Her style rankled the colony's leaders, probably because she *was* a woman who spoke her mind in a decidedly

22. Ibid., xxxix.

male-oriented society. But she was a preacher's daughter schooled by a mother who believed, in the age of the great Queen Elizabeth, that women should be just as educated and fit as the queen.

Anne taught her followers in what we today would recognize as home Bible studies. While the pastors still did all the preaching, Anne and others followed up on the sermons and discussed them "to enquire more seriously after The Lord Jesus Christ." These "conventicles" became immensely popular, not only among women, but also with husbands and other men drawn to her weekly meetings at her home.

At these meetings Hutchinson elaborated on Scripture, insisting that an "intuition of the [Holy] Spirit" was absolutely essential to salvation. Salvation was not a measure of good works, but of grace, or the freely given gift of God to man. One could not work one's way into God's grace, but once salvation was conferred on those chosen by God, then good works might follow as evidence of one's salvation.

Mainline Puritans leadership also subscribed generally to the principle that one's good works were evidence of salvation, and so good works—feeding the poor, taking care of the widows, working in the soup kitchen, etc.—were recognized as one proof of salvation. God rewarded good works with success in family, business, and life, and so if you were successful, that was *prima facie* evidence of good works, and of God's salvation.

Hutchinson and others, like Martin Luther who kicked off the Reformation a century before, claimed that *only* God's grace, freely given by God, was the path to salvation. The intervention of the Holy Spirit in their lives was the transformative agent, not works.

The controversy between Hutchinson and her friends and supporters—some of the most powerful ministers in the colony—was long called the antinomian controversy, but is now labeled the free grace controversy, since "antinomian" is probably too arcane for most modern readers.

To Winthrop and others, Hutchinson seemed to be claiming that once the Holy Spirit inhabited them, they were free from the law, or "anti-no-mian." This contradicted his sense of order and discipline, and he accused Hutchinson of blasphemy and heresy. What was really at stake was men's dominance of the Puritan colony, and a woman's claim to authority in a place reserved for men.

So they put her on trial in 1637, the principal accusation being "traducing [contradicting] the ministers,"[23] and banished her from the colony.

23. Mays, *Women in Early America*, 188.

The Boston church also held a similar "trial" in 1638 and excommunicated her for good measure.

In the trial, Winthrop failed miserably to find any true scriptural basis for the accusations and Hutchinson defended herself with great knowledge and wit. But the synod that "tried" her had already reached its conclusions before the public event.

Hutchinson packed her bags and headed down to Roger Williams's newly founded colony of Rhode Island to escape the persecution. Within a few years the hand of Massachusetts Puritans reached down even into Rhode Island and she moved further south to the Dutch colony of New Netherland, now most of New York City.

Before her new home was finished, local Indians, miffed with so many intruders and cheated by some of the Dutch and English settlers, dressed up in skins and war gear and massacred Hutchinson and all her children but one in 1643.

Winthrop crowed that God had vindicated the decision of his colony to expel such a contumacious and disturbing heretic. She had suffered several painful stillbirths and miscarriages late in life also and Winthrop threw that on her as well as proof of vindication.

If Hutchinson was guilty of anything, it was her conviction that she was a servant of only God and his Holy Spirit, not of Puritan divines such as Winthrop who viewed her as a challenge to their authority.

When it was apparent that she was losing in her trial, she struck out at her accusers in a way almost guaranteed to bring the house down on her head. "You have no power over my body, neither can you do me any harm—for I am in the hands of the eternal Jehovah, my Saviour . . . I fear none but the great Jehovah, which hath foretold me of these things, and I do verily believe that he will deliver me . . . Therefore take heed how you proceed against me—for I know that, for this you go about to do to me, God will ruin you and your posterity and this whole state."[24] Her sisters, American women, have resurrected her memory over the centuries and placed her in the pantheon of women who made a difference.

Condemned in an age of prejudice and intolerance, she helped lay the foundations of those modern precepts of liberty, freedom, and equality woven into our Constitution.

So Hutchinson and her followers, and many were important members of the Puritan community, would have none of this heretical, to her mind,

24. Morgan, *Puritan Dilemma*, 137.

relationship between work and wealth and salvation that drove much of Weber's work, coming almost three centuries after she was martyred.

The point we need to make here is that Weber's complex, sometimes tendentious, sometimes brilliant, analyses drew fire and controversy almost from the moment *The Protestant Ethic* was first published in 1905. To work was to be within God's will, so often expressed uncompromisingly and clearly in the Bible. Hutchinson had no quarrels with that. When other Puritans linked work and its results—wealth—to salvation, she clipped them off and told them "not so." Salvation only comes through faith and confession and it is a blessing given through God's grace, not the result of any work you do or wealth you accumulate.

Not only were academics and scholars curious and determined to plunge into the history of capitalism and identify its dynamics, but the debate spilled over into public forums as well. One of the most interesting fallouts was in a book written by a friend of Weber's, Georg Jellinek, and translated by Max Farrand, *The Declaration of the Rights of Man and of Citizens: A Contribution to Modern Constitutional History*, first published in translation in 1901.[25] Jellinek's argument, as summarized by Weber, was the "idea of legally establishing inalienable, inherent, and sacred rights of the individual is not of political but of religious origin." Wow, talk about turning the origins of modern, secular human rights on its head! Weber continued: "what has been held to be a work of the [French] Revolution was in reality a fruit of the Reformation and its struggles."[26]

"It first apostle," wrote Weber, in summarizing Jellinek, "was not Lafayette but Roger Williams."[27]

Jellinek makes the argument that "the template for the Declaration of the Rights of Man and of the Citizen, promulgated by the French Constituent Assembly of August 26, 1789, was not to be traced to Rousseau's *Contrat Social* (1782) but to the various Bills of Rights that issued from Virginia and elsewhere in the 1770s and early 1780s. In turn, those documents bore the impress of the uncompromising struggle for freedom of conscience that characterized the northern European Puritan movement whose seeds had fallen on American shores."[28]

---

25. Jellinek, *The Declaration of the Rights of Man*.

26. Weber, *The Protestant Ethic*, xl-xli.

27. Ibid., xl.

28. Ibid.

Here we are moving beyond the work ethic as the principal mainspring of capitalism into religion as being the mainspring of political rights given expression and form by the American Revolution and the French Revolution of the late eighteenth century. The Bible, or Scripture, assumes the role of underlying perhaps the two most significant movements in modern history: capitalism and republicanism.

As the editors of *The Protestant Ethic* note, "for Jellinek, as for Weber, the Puritan sects were radical not only in their unconditional affirmation of freedom of conscience but also in asserting that such freedom applied to everyone irrespective of the denomination to which they belonged; the Quaker and Baptist sects had helped establish a *universal*, as distinct from a local or contingent, concept of right."[29]

And, "such freedom of conscience," Weber remarked in *Economy and Society*, "may be the oldest Right of Man—as Jellinek has argued convincingly; at any rate, it is the most basic Right of Man because it comprises all ethically conditioned action and guarantees freedom from compulsion, especially from the power of the state."[30]

Weber then ties together the work ethic with freedom of conscience, both arising out of Scripture at their most basic level of creation, the word of God. "The other Rights of Man or civil rights were joined to this basic right, especially the right to pursue one's own economic interests, which includes the inviolability of individual property, the freedom of contract, and vocational choice . . . The basic Rights of Man made it possible for the capitalist to use things and men freely, just as this worldly asceticism—adopted with some dogmatic variations—and the specific discipline of the sects bred the capitalist spirit and the rational "professional" (*Berufsmensch*) who was needed by capitalism."[31]

This is heavy stuff, but important to linking Scripture, and, of course, those passages and interpretations about work and wealth, to such areas as the rise and nature of capitalism and the origins of political rights and liberty of conscience.

There is another dimension to work that we explore in the next chapter. After lifting work up, largely from scriptural passages, to something noble and directly in God's will, we need to examine why work over the centuries, especially manual labor, working with one's hands, was so despised as

29. Ibid., xli.
30. Ibid.
31. Ibid.

demeaning and not fit for those who ruled or governed. And, ironically, it came to pass that the depreciation of work took place in a very pronounced fashion directly in a Christian society, especially during the Middle Ages.

Questions for Discussion

- Why do we work?
- What is the connection between the ethics of Protestantism and the emergence of the spirit of modern capitalism?
- What was the Protestant work ethic?
- Why did Anne Hutchinson get in so much trouble with her fellow Puritans?

6

How Work Got To Be a Dirty Word

Now, lest you buy hook, line, and sinker into the "work is noble and God-given" philosophy so well described in the above chapters and even mandated in Scripture—and which I subscribe to wholeheartedly—let's examine in this chapter a bit of the history of work, especially, but not limited to, manual labor over the course of history. Work, especially common manual labor, like in farming, tending the sheep, brickmaking, the tasks of the "workingman" came to be deprecated among the upper classes, the "higher estates" in the language of Europe of the Middle Ages, the military, and even the clergy. How did this happen? And has it changed in the modern (today's) age? Does a high-flying techie with an advanced engineering degree from Stanford in Silicon Valley working for Google or Apple think less of a migrant laborer picking lettuce in the San Joaquin Valley of California?

We make this examination not to demean work, but to be able to put work not only into a Christian framework, but also into the framework of the world, often at odds with the structures and principles of Christianity.

How have attitudes towards work changed over the ages?[1] Doesn't, in fact, everything change over the years? Yes and no. Everything changes, except for Scripture. People may interpret Scripture differently over the ages, and in different cultures, but it stays the same. Attitudes towards work, like interpreting Scripture, have not always been the same.

First of all, let's remind ourselves of what Scripture says about work. Paul, in writing to the Thessalonians, was, as almost always, very direct: "The one who is unwilling to work shall not eat."[2] There is nothing complicated about that instruction. Keep this in mind as we study attitudes towards work over the ages below. I have added italics occasionally to

---

1. http://workethic.coe.uga.edu/history.htm.
2. 2 Thess 3:10.

emphasize the points. Where italics occur in the original Scripture, I point that out.

Paul also directly links work to obedience to God in a passage immediately preceding the one above in his second letter to the Thessalonians: "In the name of the Lord Jesus Christ, we command you, brothers and sisters, to keep away from every believer who *is idle and disruptive* and does not live according to the teaching you received from us."[3] To live according to the teaching that Paul gave them is to work for a living. To be idle, and so disruptive, is an offense to God. Again, Paul is often very straightforward.

In the Old Testament, Ecclesiastes holds much truth. "The *sleep of the laborer is sweet, whether they eat little or much,* but as for the rich, their abundance permits them no sleep."[4] This passage speaks as much to wealth as it does to work, but that the sleep of the laborer is sweet leaves little doubt that a "job well done" leads to satisfaction, to peace, to sleeping in peace. On the other hand, the more things you have, the more wealth you generate, the more homes you have, the more "disposable income" you have, the more worries that come with it. "*Better is a little with the fear of the Lord than great treasure and trouble with it.*"[5]

Proverbs always drive points home, and work is no different. "*Lazy hands make for poverty,* but diligent hands bring wealth."[6] Of course, one can work hard to make money illegally—like robbery, cheating, and a thousand other ways to do it—and Proverbs addresses that to: "The wages of the righteous is life, but *the earnings of the wicked are sin and death.*"[7] Proverbs 11:1 directly addresses cheats and liars: "The *Lord detests dishonest scales,* but accurate weights find favor with him." Or, "better is a little with righteousness than large income with injustice."[8]

If you are in to saving from the earnings of your work, try this one for confirmation: "Dishonest money dwindles away, but whoever gathers money little by little makes it grow."[9] As we consider work, savings, the fruits of our work, another question, a big one, rises. Who are you working for?

3. 2 Thess 3:6.
4. Eccl 5:12.
5. Prov 15:16.
6. Prov 10:4.
7. Prov 10:16.
8. Prov 16:8.
9. Prov 13:11.

Are you working for God? For yourself? For your master? Or, update it a bit, for your employer today, be it a small bakery or IBM, or the local sheriff's office, or the FBI, or the local school system, or an auto parts supplier, or the coal mine? Or maybe you are your own boss, working to keep your small company going and growing, or working to keep a giant corporation in profits and the shareholders satisfied? Who are you working for?[10]

Paul, as usual, clarifies it for us as to who we *should* be working for in a passage from his letter to the Colossians: "Whatever you do, work at it with all your heart, as working for the Lord, not for human masters."[11] This is a tough admonition, let's admit it. Not all of us love our work. Perhaps most of us, in fact, work only because we have to.

In the beginning, man didn't have too much work to do in the garden of Eden, other than tend the garden and name the plants and animals as God created them. But it was a form of work and we can surmise that God gave man something he needed to be responsible for. The big picture on work is that since man was created in God's image and God worked to bring the world into creation, he naturally enough gave man the gift of work also. "The Lord God took the man *and put him in the Garden of Eden to work it and take care of it.* And the Lord God commanded the man, 'You are free to eat from any tree in the garden; but you must not eat from the tree of the knowledge of good and evil, for when you eat from it you will certainly die.'"[12]

Most of you know the story, but if you don't or forgot, here's a summary. Adam and Eve *did* eat from the tree of the knowledge of good and evil, and so disobeyed God. Before they could bite the fruit from the other forbidden tree in the garden—the tree of life—and live forever, God expelled them from Eden.

> To Adam he said, "Because you listened to your wife and ate fruit from the tree about which I commanded you, 'You must not eat from it,'
>
> Cursed is the ground because of you;
> through painful toil you will eat food from it
> all the days of your life.
> It will produce thorns and thistles for you,

10. A nice site on scriptural passages on work is http://christianity.about.com/od/Bible-Verses/a/Work-Bible-Verses.htm.

11. Col 3:23.

12. Gen 2:15–17.

and you will eat the plants of the field.
By the sweat of your brow
you will eat your food
until you return to the ground,
since from it you were taken;
for dust you are
and to dust you will return."[13]

One can take some important lessons from God's message to man. One, man disobeyed God and there were consequences for disobedience. Two, man must now really turn to and labor hard on his land forever to make it yield the food to sustain his life. And, three, man will return in death to the dust from which he was made.

We may draw some preliminary conclusions here as we move more deeply into exploring attitudes towards work over the ages.

Work is hard if it is to be fruitful, and by fruitful we think metaphorically. You can be designing some new app for computers right now, but I can guarantee, it if is to be successful—fruitful—it is hard work. Work can be joyful and fulfilling, but is never easy. As I composed, for example, for this book, it was hard work. When I till my garden for spring planting, it is both work *and* fulfilling. God did not curse us indiscriminately or whimsically; that came through Adam's disobedience. But he did punish Adam, and we inherited that punishment called sin, until the "second Adam," Jesus Christ, came and removed the sin and restored us to the promise of life everlasting.

In the meantime, until Jesus returns a second time, we are stuck with work as a means of fulfilling God's will, rather than simply taking care of the garden of Eden and naming animals, the "work" God assigned Adam in the beginning.

If you are not a believer in the inerrancy of the Bible as truth divinely revealed, or, to put it another way, think the story of the garden of Eden is a nice fairy tale invented by the ancient Hebrews, and we get to pick and choose to believe about what "really" happened in the past, or what was "really" said, read on nevertheless. The history of work is dealt with empirically as well as spiritually in this book, and they more often intersect than conflict. In other words, while you may not believe that the world was created by God in six days, and on the seventh he rested (see the first three chapters of the book of Genesis), you have to accept that at some point in time the universe as we know it was created, whether you subscribe to the

13. Gen 3:17–19.

big bang theory or some other theory. It could have happened a gazillion years ago, or a maybe 6,000 years ago, or 200,000 years ago. The universe and man were created, presumably at vastly different times, and man has to work to live, whether he got thrown out of the garden of Eden by God for disobedience, or just from the natural laws that prevail in the world. Virtually nothing is created, grown, tilled, watered, mined, refined, produced, or invented except through the work of man.

What were Hebrew attitudes towards work? What about the ancient Greeks whose rise as a civilization more or less paralleled the latter centuries of the Hebrew nation? The Greeks, and their disciples the Romans, represent much of Western thought, of which we are part of.

We can easily see from the many Scriptures we have considered so far that it was necessary to work to prevent poverty and destitution. No work, no way, no food. This attitude carries right through to the New Testament, through the fall of the Roman Empire and the rise of medieval Europe. We examine attitudes towards work in that period towards the end of this chapter.

It is clear that Jews considered work part of God's divine plan for man. This is made very clear by returning to Scripture. Exodus 20:9–10: "Six days you shall labor and do all your work, but the seventh day is a Sabbath to the Lord your God. On it you shall not do any work, neither you, nor your son or daughter, nor your male or female servant, nor your animals, nor any foreigner residing in your towns."

As the Rabbi Louis Jacobs wrote in his *The Jewish Religion: A Companion*, work is "part of the divine plan for man."[14] He wrote that while it is not part of the 600 plus commandments, or *mitzvah*, a strict religious obligation, its opposite, idleness, is not approved by Jewish moralists. Even with this caveat—kind of a legal legerdemain—it is clear that a "high value is placed on work in the Jewish ethic. Human dignity is enhanced when man sustains himself by his own efforts."[15] Or, as another Jewish writer observed, the rabbis "saw no virtue in poverty."[16] Poverty was often viewed as a result of the failure to work, and so work was not only a virtue, but also a way to avoid poverty. The Hebrews did not lift up or find any virtue in poverty, such as occurred later in some areas of Christianity, especially the monastic movement. Rabbis, like the Apostle Paul was training to be before

14. Jacobs, *The Jewish Religion*; Jacobs, "Work in Jewish Thought."
15. Jacobs, "Work in Jewish Thought."
16. Eisenberg, *What the Rabbis Said*, 142.

his conversion to becoming a follower of Jesus, worked to make a living, often as artisans, like Paul who was a tentmaker.

Another element in the Jewish attitude towards work was that a "man's work has to be beneficial to society."[17] This expands the Judaic interpretation of the meaning of work quite a bit. Work, in this way of thinking, is part of the collective experience of man, or we are all in this together.

"Well known is the Talmudic tale (BT Ta'anit 23a) of the saint who saw an old man planting trees. 'Why do you plant the trees since you will never enjoy the fruit?' the saint asked, to be given the unanswerable reply (from the Jewish point of view): 'I found trees planted by my ancestors from which I enjoyed the fruit. Surely, it is my duty to plant trees that those who come after me might enjoy their fruit.'"[18] That story needs no interpretation.

Working did not always lead to wealth of course. Some get stuck somewhere between poverty and wealth, what we today call—loosely—the middle class.

While we are on work in this chapter, let's take a quick look at what work produces, sometimes abundantly—wealth. What obligations do we have to the poor, especially among those who God has favored with wealth, or, at the very least, more than they need for mere subsistence?

Among ancient Hebrews, a word exists called *Tzedakah*, which is usually taken to signify "charity," but which literally means "justice" or "righteousness."[19] *Tzedakah* refers to the religious obligation to do what is right and just, while traditionally charity is thought of as a spontaneous giving out of good will and generosity. We need not tarry into the detailed meanings of these words. What is important to recognize is that Judaism bequeathed to Christianity one of the cardinal principles of the universal church, to help the poor. In Judaism the great Spanish rabbi and Jewish teacher, Maimonides (1135–1204), wrote that "the highest form [of *tzedakah*] is to give a gift, loan, or partnership that will result in the recipient supporting himself instead of living upon others."[20] Or, as the old Chinese proverb put it, "give a man a fish and you feed him for a day; teach a man to fish and you feed him for a lifetime." Since fishing is a form of work—and several of Jesus' disciples were fisherman—let's turn at this point to a wider consideration of work and what attitudes toward work societies, from the

17. Jacobs, "Work in Jewish Thought."
18. Ibid.
19. Donin, *To Be a Jew*, 48.
20. Ibid.

ancient until today, are important for us to consider. While we have focused on what the Bible says about work in this short study, work is a fundamental part of life across all cultures and religions, and we can compare Christian attitudes towards work better within the larger framework of all men across time.

In a truly encyclopedic study of work across history, the anthropologist Herbert Applebaum defined work: "work uses the things and materials of nature to fashion tools with which to make objects, grow food, and control the living creatures and forces of nature to satisfy human needs and wants."[21] Another word for work is "occupation," emphasizing it is what people do to earn a living and sustain life.

And let's be up front with an observation related to the author of this excellent study on work. While he does devote a chapter to the attitudes toward work among Jews and Christians, and he does include the Christian religious attitudes towards work through the centuries since the coming of Christianity, he does not—as most Christian readers will—place God at the center of his study of work.[22] Applebaum's bias is that work is largely a function of man's determination to live and prosper among the resources of the earth through his own creativity and imagination, omitting by and large the role of God, although certainly not the influence of Jewish and Christian thinking on work. However, that is but a caveat, or caution, as we proceed to examine work, as determined through the intense and thoughtful study of the subject in his book.

Curiously, he expresses biblical principles related to work sometimes, but in a secular fashion. Here, for example, is his view of what most Christians would understand as a fundamental principle expressed in the word "stewardship."[23]

"Viewing work as aiming for the satisfaction of human needs can be a problem," Applebaum writes. "This view gives humans the sanction to use the natural world for their own needs. [This is biblical actually; see for example Gen 1:28]. It contains the danger that such an idea sees the natural world as exploitable rather than as an aid to human endeavor to be used

---

21. Applebaum, *The Concept of Work*, x. The book is 645 pages in length.

22. See chapter 6, "The Attitudes Toward Work Among the Jews and Among the Christians," in Applebaum, *The Concept of Work*, 179ff.

23. See for example "Four Principles of Biblical Stewardship" at the Institute for Faith, Work & Economics website: http://blog.tifwe.org/four-principles-of-biblical-steward-ship, in which the following passages explain the concept of stewardship of resources in Scripture: Ps 24; Deut 8:17–18; the parable of the talents, and Col 3:23–24, for example.

with care."[24] We are, in fact, caretakers of all God has provided us with, and so stewards with all that implies.

Two patterns emerge, Applebaum writes, from his study of work. "One is that the aristocracy, the literati, and the men in power have traditionally had contempt for those who must work. The good life was the life of leisure, free from the constraint of work," although "the independent farmer was somewhat of an exception."[25] We'll return to this below, since the church had, in fact, something to do with cultivating this most anti-biblical attitude towards work, especially during the Middle Ages, or medieval period in Western history.

And a second theme that emerged from Applebaum's studies is that "people who worked may not have shared the contempt with which they were held by the powerful and the literate."[26] These are the people who left no written history, largely because of illiteracy, but often left tremendous testaments to their brilliant work (like in the cathedrals for example) and to their self-worth and self-respect.

Applebaum begins his study of work in the ancient society of Greece, or the world of the great poet Homer, thus "Homeric world," circa 850 BC. In this period of the "nonmarket culture," work "is imbedded in all the activities of the society and therefore acceptable to all ranks and groups, nobles as well as commoners."[27] Everyone worked—nobles and commoners alike.

The three "noblest" forms of work in the Greek city-states were agriculture and the art of war, according to Socrates, while religion was the third profession of this triangle. Governing the state, or the *polis*, was equally important, but not equated directly with work. This of course is what we consider most politicians to be in Washington. Sorry, couldn't resist editorializing a bit.

In any case, to properly govern, both Socrates and Plato felt a "life free from the compulsions of work [were conditions] for a life of virtue and therefore [were] preconditions for good leadership and good government."[28] Plato especially takes up on this theme in his *Republic*, claiming, among other things, that "any kind of work that interfered with the leisure neces-

---

24. Applebaum, *The Concept of Work*, xi.

25. Ibid., xiii

26. Ibid.

27. Ibid., 9.

28. Ibid., 35, see also pp 60ff for a fuller discussion of the qualifications to rule and/ or govern.

sary for the practice of the art of government was a disqualification for membership in his governing class."[29] Other Greeks, such as Protagoras, weren't quite so snobby about those fit to govern. He thought smiths and shoemakers, for example, could share profitably in governing. So, unless we get too straitjacketed here, there were differences of opinion among the ancients on what constituted work, and how different work contributed to the well-being and government of the state. What is important to underscore is that all agreed that work was necessary for the individual and for the collective whole. Not to work, as the Hebrews agreed in the same time period, was scandalous and an affront to man and God.

Yet, even given the above understanding, there was already at work (sorry about the play on words) a growing prejudice *against* manual labor. Let's explore this a bit since it becomes part of Western attitudes towards work over the ages. Both Plato and Socrates argued that those who rule should be set aside and trained to rule, and they could not be craftsmen (or other workmen as civilization became more complicated with a growing diversity of what constituted work) as well. Plato's argument is rather weak, that the craftsman's mind and body was ruined by the manual arts and so disqualified them to rule, but Socrates, and most of the ancients— except for Plato—almost invariably excluded the farmer from this Platonic condemnation, for their occupation trained them not only to be good citizens and good soldiers, but they also provided the food and sustenance for civilization to exist.

Plato doesn't think as much of the farmer and his occupation, or his ability to share in governing the state. Farming doesn't train men in the art of government, nor does the farmer have the leisure to acquire those skills while out there plowing the lower forty. Furthermore, most men were proficient at only one skill or pursuit, and once they learned it, they needed to stay with it. Plato would not have fit into modern American life, so given to change, mobility, and inconstancy in many areas.

That Plato contributed to the strain of thought of those "who believed in the inferiority of the people who must work to feed, clothe, and house others who ruled over them" cast Plato in the role of helping produce the "first comprehensive diagnosis of the human condition in Western tradition," or more simply put, defining social attitudes between different forms

29. Ibid., 61.

of work.[30] Or, even more simply, the rich and/or privileged looked down their noses at the working slobs.

In our investigation of the role of wealth and work in Christianity, this becomes important since work remains central in Scripture (remember Scripture does not change) but other phenomenon and changes in cultures and civilizations *do* impose sometimes radically different attitudes towards work and wealth. Applebaum captures well the dilemma defined by Plato. "The viewpoint of Plato that those who must work are unfit to rule and that work is demeaning to the spirit is a view which has existed among the wealthy and the few at the top of society [the famous 1% of today] through-out all ages, including the present one." The author concludes that "it has not been fully overcome," ignoring, either out of commission or omission, the Judeo-Christian response.[31]

Aristotle, the giant among Greek philosophers still quoted today, tended to agree with Plato. For citizens of the city-state to engage success-fully in the higher callings of war, politics, and the art of government, they needed to be free to study music, philosophy, art, and the like which "could be mastered only by education and training which, in turn, could only be available to the man of leisure."[32] There you have it. The ultimate justifica-tion for the "leisure society."

Now, if you aren't doing the same calculations I'm doing here, you've missed something. Today leisure *does not* lead to a deeper understanding and appreciation of music, art, mathematics, history, philosophy, science, or computer programming. You can fill in the blank yourselves as to how modern man spends his "leisure" time. This is not what Plato or Aristotle meant. Leisure in their definition translates into "work," if we agree that study, contemplation, reflection, analysis, reading, writing, and doing ge-ometry all constitute work.

"As did Plato before him," Applebaum writes, "Aristotle did not believe that working people, *even farmers*, could be trained to rule the state, nor could they be truly good citizens if they were required to work."[33]

---

30. Ibid., 61–62.

31. Ibid., 63. Although in Applebaum's defense he does have an entire chapter to-wards the attitudes towards work among Jews and Christians. But it is more explanatory than hortatory.

32. Ibid., 64.

33. Ibid., 67, italics added.

On the other hand, the Stoic philosophy that dominated Hellenistic thinking at the time Christianity emerged, *did* attribute "a positive value to work."[34] The concept that the craftsman and tradesman, as well as the farmer, contributed positively to society gained credence. And, curiously enough, perhaps the greatest Stoic philosopher of the era, Seneca, lived contemporaneously with the beginning of the Christian era (4 BC—AD 65), and much of Seneca's teachings remarkably parallel much of Christianity's early teachings.

"A great fortune is a great slavery."

"God is the universal substance in existing things. He comprises all things. He is the fountain of all being. In Him exists everything that is."

"It is the sign of a great mind to dislike greatness, and to prefer things in measure to things in excess."[35]

We return below to wealth within Scripture, a slippery rascal that lures but entraps us at the same time. It is no wonder that Jesus addressed so many of his parables to wealth and money while the nobility of all work—especially fishermen who Jesus recruited as disciples—was almost taken for granted.

After Greece came Rome, although Roman society and culture were imbued with Hellenistic thinking and values. And the philosopher, politician, and orator Marcus Tullius Cicero (106–43 BC) was the foremost spokesman for his time. He tended to accept Platonic and Aristotelian attitudes towards work. He didn't like "vulgar" professionals like tax-gatherers and usurers who generally incurred people's ill will. This attitude is probably still prevalent in some circles today. How many people like to pay big interests on a loan, and how many like the IRS?

Cicero had, in fact, a pecking order of what he styled vulgar work, some more vulgar, some less, from hired workmen for manual labor, retail merchants, fishmongers, butchers, cooks, and fishermen.[36] Acceptable professions or work "from which no small benefit to society is derived," included medicine, architecture, teaching, and large scale merchants. Agriculture remained at the top of the heap, "none more profitable, none more delightful, none more becoming to a freeman."[37]

---

34. Ibid., 91

35. http://www.brainyquote.com/quotes/authors/l/lucius_annaeus_seneca.html.

36. Applebaum, *The Concept of Work*, 95, quoting directly from Cicero.

37. Ibid.

So, summarizing Cicero, most activities related to commerce, trade, and manufacturing were deemed inferior by Rome's aristocracy, while political and military activities and agriculture were esteemed.[38]

And at the core of work at the top of heap was reading. "Read at every wait," he wrote "Read at all hours; read within leisure; read in times of labor; read as one goes in; read as one goes out. The task of the educated mind is simply put: read to lead."[39] This is patently good advice for any society, but most especially a literate society where information and knowledge is transferred by reading. If labor is work, then reading and learning were most discernibly work, although we can read for pleasure as well, obviously.

In Applebaum's conclusion to the section on work in the ancient world he discerns what I consider a pretty startling, provocative, and original insight. There was *no* word for work as we know it in Homeric society because work and life were one. "There was a unity," Applebaum observed, "between work and all aspects of culture in those early days that, in later centuries . . . was fractured and ruptured. This unity was never to be restored in the history of Western civilization, except perhaps for the self-contained communities of monastic orders [which we return to below since they form an integral part of Christendom], the utopian experiments in nineteenth century America, or the kibbutzim movement in Israel."[40]

The dignity and worth of agricultural work on one's own land always trumped any other form of work in importance in the ancient world. It was from the yeoman farmer that sprang the warriors who defended and spread Roman civilization. That slavery permeated the empire and peasants did much of the work, in reality, did not disturb the power of the idea or myth of the farmer or woodsman who could heft a sword or lance as well as plow the land and hew timber.

Another persistent thread from the times of the Roman Empire was the denigration of work done by the lower classes. Manual work was looked down upon by the elites. But a new way of looking at the world of work and wealth entered the equation in the first century: the rise of Christianity.

Applebaum devotes an entire chapter towards the attitudes toward work among Jews and early Christians and while there is some repetition in his chapter and the chapters in this book, it is worth following his thread, albeit briefly.

38. Ibid., 95–96.

39. https://www.goodreads.com/author/quotes/13755.Cicero.

40. Applebaum, *The Concept of Work*, 167.

What Christians perhaps take for granted was indeed new among the ancients: the Hebrews worshipped a God who *worked*. He brought the world into being through his word, he worked six days creating it, and on the seventh he took a break. This is, of course, all described in the book of Genesis.

Not only did the Hebrews, and by extension, Christians, have a God who worked, but he also esteemed agriculture and endowed the land which the Jews worked as sacred. As Arthur T. Geoghegan observed in his book, *The Attitude Towards Labor in Early Christianity and Ancient Culture*, "the land which they worked was sacred . . . farmwork was . . . a service performed for God . . . [and] the produce itself was the gift of God."[41]

Even men who worked for wages—generally despised in Hellenistic and Roman cultures—were given grace. One reads in Deuteronomy 24:14–15: "Do not take advantage of a hired worker who is poor and needy, whether that worker is a fellow Israelite or a foreigner residing in one of your towns. Pay them their wages each day before sunset, because they are poor and are counting on it. Otherwise they may cry to the Lord against you, and you will be guilty of sin."

Furthermore, in the Old Testament many, if not all, of the great Hebrew leaders worked with their hands. Gideon was threshing wheat in a winepress when the Angel of the Lord appeared to him (Judg 6:11), Saul was "returning from the fields, behind his oxen," (1 Sam 11:5) David was a herdsman (1 Sam 16:11), Elisha was a farmer (1 Kgs 19:19), and so on. Everyone worked.

Rabbis also worked, some as farmers, others as woodcutters, masons, sandal makers, and so forth. "Some Rabbis," as is always the wont it seems in any culture, "argued that the study of the Torah was superior to physical work and that it was impossible to attain wisdom and be engaged in physical work."[42] In the book of *Sirach*, sometimes called the book of *Ecclesiasticus*, we find "leisure gives the scribe the chance to acquire wisdom; a man with few commitments can grow wise."[43] The author argues that the ploughman, blacksmith, potter, and all workmen and craftsmen, "all these people rely on their hands and each is skilled at his own craft." "But," and here is the "but" that is often thrown in to unravel an argument, "you will not find them in the parliament, the do not hold high rank in the assembly. They do not sit on the judicial bench, and they do not meditate on the law."

41. Geoghegan, *The Attitude Towards Labor*, 64.
42. Applebaum, *The Concept of Work*, 181.
43. *Ecclesiastic.*, 38:24

And, so they "are not remarkable for their culture or judgment, nor are they found frequenting the philosophers."[44] Applebaum suggests that late Greek Hellenism had reached even into classical Hebrew thinking, since *Ecclesiasticus* was probably written in the early second century BC. Some rabbis were almost Jeffersonian in their advice: both work and think, although some of us may think that thinking *is* work.

Rabbi Joshua b. Hananiah said, "if a man learns two paragraphs of the Law in the morning and two in the evening, and is busy at his work all the day, they reckon it to him as if he had fulfilled the whole law."[45] Another, Judah the Prince said "Get yourselves a handicraft as well as the Torah."[46] In other words, there must be a balance between working with one's hands, and working with one's mind.

But, underscoring all was the condemnation of idleness. Even those professions considered a bit unseemly or disreputable, like camel drivers, physicians, and butchers, were better than being idle. By the way, you may have figured camel drivers and butchers, the former known for their quick hands into others' possessions and the latter for their dishonesty, but physicians? They were considered too materialistic.

With the coming of Jesus, attitudes were altered somewhat, but not radically since Jesus was born a Jew and so much of Jewish culture came to permeate early Christianity. Although Jesus did not directly address work, what he taught and how he lived spoke volumes.

He surrounded himself with companions who worked. A number— Peter among them—were fishermen, and one—Matthew—was even a tax collector, someone *nobody* liked.

Even more important perhaps was the doctrine or teaching of brotherly love that fostered an equality and respect for all people, regardless of status or occupation.[47] If everyone was worthy, then so was what they did for a living. Jesus even forgave prostitutes and lent them the hand of forgiveness if they repented and started anew. Nobody was too lowly or humble or deprived or desecrated by circumstances—brought on by themselves or by the forces of the devil—not to be lifted up by Jesus.

His principal follower after his death was the Apostle Paul who was the most prominent of the very early Christian theologians, or someone

44. *Ecclesiastic.*, 28:25–34.
45. Applebaum, *The Concept of Work*, 181.
46. Ibid.
47. Ibid., 183.

who took Jesus' teachings and rendered them into a comprehensive theology. In other words, what did Jesus mean by all this teachings, and how could early Christians best preserve, enhance, and grow their faith?

Paul practiced his trade as tentmaker all the while he was traveling on his many missions to preach about Jesus. He knew that he had a right to a living from those he preached to. He devotes an entire chapter in his first letter to the Corinthians (1 Cor 9) on his rights as an apostle, which he likened to any other profession, such as soldier, winemaker, herdsman, or farmer. He asked, among other questions, rhetorically:

"Who serves as a soldier at his own expense?

"Who plants a vineyard and does not eat its grapes?

"Who tends a flock and does not drink the milk?

And then he asks, rather sharply, "If we have sown spiritual seed among you, is it too much if we reap a material harvest from you?"[48] While Paul then explains himself in a not too convincing fashion that he is doing all this for free, so as not to burden the people with his needs and get the gospel to them freely, he makes a good case for the spiritual labors of a pastor or preacher, or apostle as he preferred styling himself. This too is work.

As much as work occupied the early Christians, Jesus directed more attention on how to handle wealth, and for some really good insights we turn to an excellent study by one the premier modern historians of Christianity, Justo B. González.[49]

In his *A History of Early Christian Ideas on the Origin, Significance, and Use of Money*, he frames his study with a question: he was not interested in "how rich or how poor Christians were at a given time and place, but rather what Christians thought and taught regarding the rights and responsibilities of both rich and poor."[50] So, while trained as a theologian, González took a page or two out of economics, examining the distribution of wealth, land tenure, and the rights of the poor. And he discovered, not surprisingly, that questions associated with the economy—like wealth—are intimately related to ethics and faith, which represents a point of view which brought us to write this book in the first place.[51]

---

48. All quotes from 1 Cor 9, NIV.

49. González, *Faith and Wealth*.

50. Ibid., xiii.

51. González argues this both in his preface and retrospect, such as pg. 225ff., for example.

Virtually all of the early Christians, if we define early Christianity loosely as the first three or four centuries after Christ, agreed. Questions of faith and wealth were inseparable given the teachings of Christ and his early interpreters. And, I would argue, they still are, today in the twenty-first century.

Some thinking of the early Christians, which we examine in a bit of detail below, goes against the grain of modern thinking.

Early Christians, for example, were almost unanimously aligned against the practice of loaning money and charging interest, loosely labeled usury.[52]

Early Christians also turned the traditional meanings of rich and poor upside down. To be rich in wealth often led to being poor in virtue and poor in joy. Jesus spoke to this issue (see Matt 16:26 for just one example), and early Christian writers also borrowed from classical pagan sources, describing the seekers of wealth as "being similar to a person who is always thirsty." The theme that excessive wealth brought nothing but worry also runs like a thread through early Christianity. One can fast forward that particular snippet of wisdom to the twenty-first century. It is still valid. The more you have, the more you worry about.

While giving to the poor and taking care of the orphans and widows is a theme constant in Hebrew writings, it survived and prospered in early Christianity as well. Almsgiving and tithing were woven into the woof and warp of Christian thinking on wealth and what to do with it. And it remains a theme in modern Christianity that we deal with in several other sections of this book. As we have noted on numerous occasions, it is not so much poverty or lack of wealth that befuddles and so confounds Christians, but the acquisition and then use of wealth. It can become *the* determining factor in your lives, and that draws your focus off of God.

Wealth, all early Christians believed, should be shared, not hoarded or accumulated for its own sake. Eventually the monastic tradition grew out of this early Christian matrix of rejecting wealth altogether and embracing poverty. This stands in stark contrast to the theme we covered above: how wealth and capitalism were apparently inexorably linked by the Protestant work ethic.

Juxtapositions and even contradictions in the subject of work and wealth are, of course, not just the property of Christians. Early on, the Greeks were divided—Plato and Aristotle representing the two poles—on how the ideal state should be ordered. Plato believed that "common property should be the rule in such a state." Aristotle, on the other hand, "argued

---

52. Here and next few paragraphs, following González, *Faith and Wealth*, 226ff.

for private property." And all agreed there should be *a limit* to the wealth held by any individual, to prevent corruption.[53] The Romans tended to favor private property, but with it came wealth, and as one of the most prominent of Roman philosophers, and a contemporary of Jesus, Seneca, observed, with wealth came anxiety and fear and sorrow, worrying over keeping one's fortune and accumulating more, and, even more fearful, of losing it all.[54]

The Jewish tradition existed contemporaneously with the Greek and Roman civilizations and, of course, it was from the Hebrews that Jesus emerged. In Jewish beliefs, land—the main sort of their wealth in biblical times—belonged ultimately to God. There were certain rules governing what the Hebrews could do with their land, although this need not tarry us here.[55] Since God owned the land, it followed that "ownership of the land also meant that part of its produce had to be reserved for God, both directly through tithes and other similar duties, and indirectly by making it available to the needy."[56] The Jews argued over the details of these principles but ultimately accepted the dictum that God had a special concern for the poor, and it was the obligation of those who had land, resources, and wealth to meet the basic needs of the poor, the sojourners (or traveler), the orphans, and the widows.

The "Jesus movement" as scholars commonly refer to the times of Jesus was marked by an "unsettled atmosphere, full of fear and resentment, of crushing poverty and messianic expectations." Much of what Jesus preached about the coming kingdom of God had to do with work and wealth, and more specifically addressing socioeconomic realities, especially the gulf between the rich and the poor, the haves and the have-nots. As González so correctly noted, "themes of economic justice appear repeatedly in the preaching of Jesus and of the early movement."[57] The parables about such subjects as the talents, the unjust steward, the laborers in the vineyard, the rich young ruler, and others speak both directly and indirectly to the distribution and use of wealth. How was all this to be organized in the coming kingdom of God?

In a radical departure from the normal state of events, Jesus pronounced that the last will be the first, and the first last in Matthew 20:16. This is called the "great reversal" by students of Christianity. Or, as in a favorite tune played by George Washington's army as they received the

53. González, *Faith and Wealth*, 14.

54. Ibid., 17.

55. See ibid., 20, for some of these details.

56. Ibid.

57. Ibid., 75.

surrender of the mighty British army at Yorktown in 1781, the world was turned upside down.

And so it was with Jesus' prescriptions. "Those who are now underprivileged and oppressed," one theologian noted, "will be first in the Kingdom."[58] This was not a complex truth hidden in a parable or metaphor. In the Lucan version of the Beatitudes (6:20–26), found also Matthew's accounts of Jesus' life, Jesus very clearly spoke of what to expect in the new Kingdom of God he was inaugurating.

> Blessed are you who are poor,
> for yours is the kingdom of God.
> Blessed are you who hunger now,
> for you will be satisfied.
> Blessed are you who weep now,
> for you will laugh.
> Blessed are you when people hate you,
> when they exclude you and insult you
> and reject your name as evil,
> because of the Son of Man.
> Rejoice in that day and leap for joy, because great is your reward in
> heaven. For that is how their ancestors treated the prophets.
> But woe to you who are rich,
> for you have already received your comfort.
> Woe to you who are well fed now,
> for you will go hungry.
> Woe to you who laugh now,
> for you will mourn and weep.
> Woe to you when everyone speaks well of you.

The Beatitudes (from a Latin adjective meaning happy, fortunate, or blissful) were so contrary to the way the world works that they, in fact, have to be authentic. This strange sort of reasoning is one way to determine truth among those who interpret and study languages. The statement, or in this case, the principles stated in the Beatitudes, are so contrary that anyone writing the life of Christ would probably have edited them out, or excised them, as totally unrealistic and not believable. That they were kept, and very prominently in both the gospels of Matthew and Luke, speaks to their authenticity. Everyone at the time was familiar with them. Jesus had spoken them. We can't simply omit them because they don't fit reality. The inauguration of the kingdom of heaven by Jesus was in fact introducing a

58. Ibid., 76.

new reality, one that is important in this little primer on work and wealth in the Bible since they were so radical and contrary to the nature of man. That's because, essentially, they came from God, not man.

Okay, putting aside a little preachy moment in composing the first draft to this book, let's move along. Another one of Jesus's stories about a rich young ruler who wanted to be assured of eternal life really threw the "reversal" into a stark contrast. When the young man said he had kept all the commandments that Jesus mentioned as necessary, and asked, essentially, what more, Jesus answered. "If you want to be perfect, go, sell your possessions and give to the poor, and you will have treasure in heaven. Then come, follow me" (Matt 19:21). Give everything away? How could he do that? "When the young man heard this, he went away sad, because he had great wealth" (Matt 19:22).

The disciples were astounded, and Jesus quickly addressed them also. "Truly I tell you, it is hard for someone who is rich to enter the kingdom of heaven. Again I tell you, it is easier for a camel to go through the eye of a needle than for someone who is rich to enter the kingdom of God" (Matt 19–23–24).

The stark reality of the "great reversal" was given even deeper significance by the doctrine of "renunciation." To be able to enter the kingdom of heaven, a rich man needed not only to have a change of heart, but he also needed to renounce his wealth, and give it all away!

We are a long way from the Puritans of the sixteenth and seventeenth centuries who Max Weber saw as the central actors in the making of modern capitalism (discussed in an earlier chapter), compelled by their "Protestant work ethic" to accumulate and conserve their wealth. Their wealth, or capital as the case may be, was admittedly to be applied to the growing kingdom of God on earth, but, nonetheless, making wealth became a central component to their Christian walk.

In the story of the rich young ruler, we face a question brought on especially by a reading of Luke. "In short, Luke is dealing with the question that will later become a burning issue for Clement of Alexandria [and I might add, for other Christians across the ages]: how can the rich be saved?"[59]

The simple answer, if we follow Jesus literally, is simple: get unrich. Give away all your material possessions and follow Jesus. In today's world— and throughout the ages in fact—most of us think of such a radical prescription as impractical, unworkable, and totally at odds with the way the

59. Ibid., 79.

world works. In fact, as we see below when exploring the world of hermits and monks, quite a few Christians have embraced that alternate reality.

Another phenomenon dealing with wealth arose in the early church, and Christians have been struggling with it ever since. It is described in the second and fourth chapter of Acts. "All the believers were together and had everything in common. They sold property and possessions to give to anyone who had need" (2:44–45). And,

> All the believers were one in heart and mind. No one claimed that any of their possessions was their own, but they shared everything they had. With great power the apostles continued to testify to the resurrection of the Lord Jesus. And God's grace was so powerfully at work in them all that there were no needy persons among them. For from time to time those who owned land or houses sold them, brought the money from the sales and put it at the apostles' feet, and it was distributed to anyone who had need (4:32–35)

The Greek word used most frequently to describe this community of sharers is *koinonia*, which has several meanings, among them fellowship, brotherhood, and, as González writes, "it also means partnership, as in a common business venture."[60] Following González loosely, it means more than fellowship, but also sharing, not only of goods but feelings. Why all this fuss on *koinonia*, which is the word used in Acts 2:42, usually translated as fellowship to describe the community of believers who shared everything?

At the root of the discussion is whether these early Christians really shared everything—so described very clearly in Acts—and so constituted a form of social and religious cooperative where everything was owned as a whole, or was this just an anomaly in a society—largely Roman in law and institutions—where private property and ownership was the norm? Or, we can put it even more simply, were these early Christians practicing a form of socialism or—shudder—communism—rather than behaving like good little private property owners, the predecessors, by hundreds of years, of the proto-capitalists who Max Weber described?

It is not an unimportant question as we consider the significance and attitudes towards wealth in the Bible. And it cannot simply be buried as an abstract principle that was expressed only by a few radical Christians in the early church.

González argues that this was not the principle of "renunciation," which runs so prominently through the book of Luke, but, rather, "what

60. Ibid., 82.

is described in Acts is a community where people relinquish their possessions, not for the sake of renunciation, but for the sake of those in need."[61]
This is largely true, and a principle we discuss below, but González twists
logic around somewhat to avoid the central question: was the sharing of
resources a true representation of how these early Christians treated their
resources and their wealth? The answer is, yes, they threw their resources
together and so temporarily abandoned the principle of private property.
But, as González so convincingly argues, they did it not simply to satisfy
some stand-alone principle like "renunciation," but rather to help the poor
and those in the early church who *needed* the help. Here the principle of
helping the poor, the widows, the dispossessed, the orphans, and others
descends directly in a line from Hebrew laws and practices.

And, in a direct fashion, the principle of tithing is preserved from Judaism to Christianity, with the concomitant understanding that Christian charity and compassion, through material gifts and supports, was not a choice,
but a mandate from God. Wealth takes on a new meaning. It is not just to
provide for one's welfare, shelter, and well-being—all very much approved
in Scripture in the many passages on work—but it is to share with fellow
Christians, to, in fact, live in line with certain principles, so well described in
the following passage from the second book of James. "What good is it, my
brothers and sisters, if someone claims to have faith but has no deeds? Can
such faith save them? Suppose a brother or a sister is without clothes and
daily food. If one of you says to them, 'Go in peace; keep warm and well fed,'
but does nothing about their physical needs, what good is it? In the same way,
faith by itself, if it is not accompanied by action, is dead" (James 2:14–17).

The easiest and most efficient way of helping others is obviously by
employing your wealth to do so, but just about every time the subject appears in the early church, it comes with bells and whistles, warnings about
the trapdoors opening for the rich to step into and disappear into the
depths of black eternity.[62] The Old Testament speaks very directly to the
same issue: wealth and its entrapments.[63]

61. Ibid., 82.

62. Of course, perhaps the most demanding way to help your fellow Christian is by
giving her your time, but that is another subject.

63. One excellent web site, a page in OpenBible.info entitled "51 Bible Verses About
Money Management": http://www.openbible.info/topics/money_management. It takes
you to over fifty (I added at least one as of April, 2014) passages on wealth, many leading
one to some thoughtful considerations about wealth and our management and attitudes
towards wealth and riches.

One prominent theme is summarized by the old—and common—adage, "you can't take it with you." How true. When Howard Hughes, legendary entrepreneur and founder of Trans World Airlines among other ventures, died, someone asked, "How much did he leave?" And a quick wit answered, "All of it."

Psalms 49:5–12, calls our attention to this reality in some vivid language that leaves little to the imagination. Your wealth does not go with you, no matter how powerful it apparently endowed some when living.

> Why should I fear when evil days come,
> when wicked deceivers surround me—
> those who trust in their wealth
> and boast of their great riches?
> No one can redeem the life of another
> or give to God a ransom for them—
> the ransom for a life is costly,
> no payment is ever enough—
> so that they should live on forever
> and not see decay.
> For all can see that the wise die,
> that the foolish and the senseless also perish,
> leaving their wealth to others.
> Their tombs will remain their houses forever,
> their dwellings for endless generations,
> though they had named lands after themselves.
> People, despite their wealth, do not endure;
> they are like the beasts that perish.

This chapter in Psalms continues in even more somber and almost morbid language.

> This is the fate of those who trust in themselves,
> and of their followers, who approve their sayings.
> They are like sheep and are destined to die;
> death will be their shepherd
> (but the upright will prevail over them in the morning).
> Their forms will decay in the grave,
> far from their princely mansions.
> But God will redeem me from the realm of the dead;
> he will surely take me to himself.
> Do not be overawed when others grow rich,
> when the splendor of their houses increases;
> for they will take nothing with them when they die,

their splendor will not descend with them.
Though while they live they count themselves blessed—
and people praise you when you prosper—
they will join those who have gone before them,
who will never again see the light of life (Ps 49:13–19).

The message in these passages from Psalms 49 is clear enough without my commentary to urge you on to consider their meaning. What I would underscore, however, is verse 15 above, "But God will redeem me from the realm of the dead; he will surely take me to himself." This looks forward to the coming of Jesus Christ, our redeemer. He, in fact, redeemed us from death by the atonement on the cross, and so fulfilled this prophecy in the Old Testament.

In a way, it also prefigures another famous principle in the New Testament expressed by Paul in his letter to his young disciple Timothy: "For the love of money is a root of all kinds of evil. Some people, eager for money, have wandered from the faith and pierced themselves with many griefs" (1 Tim 6:10). Paul does not condemn money, or wealth, but how the love of it causes one grief and to be disconnected from God's will. The Old and New Testaments are directly connected in the above passages. Psalms 62 is poetic in the expression of these sentiments.

Surely the lowborn are but a breath,
the highborn are but a lie.
If weighed on a balance, they are nothing;
together they are only a breath.
Do not trust in extortion
or put vain hope in stolen goods;
though your riches increase,
do not set your heart on them.
One thing God has spoken,
two things I have heard:
"Power belongs to you, God,
and with you, Lord, is unfailing love";
and, "You reward everyone
according to what they have done" (62:9–12).

Repeating a theme can sometimes be tiresome and unnecessary. But repeating a theme drawn from Scripture is never so.[64] González does a good

64. I am reminded, of course, of correcting children every time they stray or go wrong. As parents, how many times have we done this? I am not suggesting we are all children in need of constant correction, but Jesus *did* say that sometimes we need to

job of summarizing the theme of wealth and the hand of God. "The theme of a reward for those who do not cling to their wealth," he writes, "but employ it for good deeds, sounds most clearly in 1 Timothy 6:17–19: 'Command those who are rich in this present world not to be arrogant nor to put their hope in wealth, which is so uncertain, but to put their hope in God, who richly provides us with everything for our enjoyment. Command them to do good, to be rich in good deeds, and to be generous and willing to share. In this way they will lay up treasure for themselves as a firm foundation for the coming age, so that they may take hold of the life that is truly life.'"[65]

And González notes, "here we find, not only the notion that by making good use of treasures on earth we can acquire treasures in heaven, but also the contrast between the two kinds of riches. Some are 'rich in this world,' others are 'rich in good deeds.' While the two are not mutually exclusive, they are quite distinct."[66] The connection between them—possibly the most important—is that to give to the poor, to be generous in charity, to help the needy, to reach out to other Christians, it sure helps to have resources. This is a nicer way of saying something like "money," which sounds a bit tawdry after considering all of the injunctions above against the rich and the wealthy. But if one is to give to the poor and lend a hand to your fellow Christians, or even to non-believers, it stands to reason that you need to have something to give or provide.

We can beat this horse about the reversal or the alternate reality, turning wealth and poverty upside down, but it is important because a sector of the early Christian community did embrace poverty as an ideal. We are writing, of course, of the monastic movement that we mentioned in the chapter on "Name It and Claim It" above. Furthermore, during the reign of the Emperor Constantine, a dramatic reversal in the fortunes of the church occurred, one that would have reverberations on the themes of work and wealth, but especially the latter, across the centuries, even to today.

In AD 313 Constantine stopped the persecution of the Christian church, and in 325, he went a step further, making Christianity the "official" religion of the empire. In the space of three centuries, Christianity went from a small, persecuted sect of Judaism on the fringes of the Roman Empire to being the official religion of that mighty empire of the ancient world. It was a remarkable transition.

---

listen and hear with the innocence of children to hear his true message.

65. González, *Faith and Wealth*, 87.

66. Ibid., 87–88.

For the church it meant acquiring new prestige and wealth. The emperor himself became the head of the church, or, at the very least, the leading patron to challenge the growing stature of the papacy as the spiritual head of the church. And, as González noted, the sudden influx of wealth and power affected the life of the church. "One of the most obvious consequences," he rightly noted, "was an enormous increase in the resources now available to the church for charitable work."[67] While doing good now stretched across a wide spectrum of society in need, the church also began to grow in worldly splendor.

The physical and temporal growth of the church followed over the next 1000 years, with the material assets of the church—cathedrals, monasteries, lands, benefices, etc.—expanding so that by the Late Middle Ages, or the fourteenth and fifteenth centuries, the name "church" was almost synonymous with wealth, especially surrounding the institution of the papacy.

As we track the church, and the subjects of work, but especially of wealth, into the post-Roman empire Middle Ages, González summarized the view well. "Two different ways of being Christian," he wrote, "were now open: one the more radical way of the monastics, including voluntary poverty and the commonality of goods; the other the common way of the majority of Christians, for whom the connection between faith and wealth receded into the background."[68]

And, in an interesting forward to a period and theme we have already covered somewhat in the sections above on wealth generation and the Protestant work ethic. "When the Protestant Reformation did away with monasticism, rejecting what it took to be an attempt to gain heaven by works, it also did away with what had been monasticism's reminder to the entire church of the need for obedience in economic matters."[69] The rise of the Puritans and the Protestant work ethic responded to that need to rethink wealth in both spiritual and worldly terms, reconciling, or at the least, trying to reconcile the two.

Returning to the theme of work, we know that the Apostle Paul worked as a tentmaker and he worked to meet his needs, and those of others. In his second letter to the Thessalonians, Paul spoke directly to issues of work and idleness. He mentioned his own work ethic as one worth imitating, and if one chose not to work, then he chose not to eat. Work and earn your living

67. Ibid., 153.
68. Ibid., 166.
69. Ibid.

was his admonition.[70] And he equated work directly with "doing what is good" for good measure.

He equated work broadly with independence and self-respect, and a means to economic freedom.[71] And as one worked, one usually generated more than was necessary for living; that surplus becomes an excellent source for Christian charity and so providing for the needy. Working, indeed, endowed one with more than money and resources. It gave one a sense of dignity and value, as an individual and in the community.

Work and the accumulation of resources—sometimes just enough and sometimes more than enough, or wealth—leads to another important conclusion about life among the early Christians, and one can argue even among many Christians today. Life in the church was more than "in," but also "for" the church, if by the church we mean all its members, rich and poor, men and women, slave and free. A general recognition that they were all in this endeavor together reminds one of the old adage, "one for all and all for one," usually associated to the famous three musketeers of Alexandre Dumas's novel of the same name. By the same token, when Christians participate in a wide variety of church activities today—Sunday morning services, Sunday evening services, Wednesday night study groups, traveling together, child care, and the list goes on considerably—they are making the church part of their life, or, conversely, the church is becoming their life, as it was among early Christians. And work and the generation of resources were two of the glues that bonded individuals together as the body of Christ.

A character of work which has plagued Christians from the very beginning had to do with the different attitudes towards work held by Christians of different class and caste. Did Christian society reflect society in general, often rigidly divided between free and slave, poor and rich, noble and base for example, or did Christian principles argue otherwise, for the equality of all? Today, the same issues divide us. Are the rich and well-educated and people of influence, old families and culture, better than the poor, the street person, the prisoner, the illiterate, and the outcast? Think of your own church for a second. Does it cater to all, or does it cater to a particular type of person, known by wealth or career or family name?

While there exist examples of Christian society imitating the pagan world that they inhabited, Christian pastors, theologians, and teachers argued from Scripture and the life of Christ that the working classes and the

70. 2 Thess 3:6–13.

71. Applebaum, *The Concept of Work*, 184–85.

poor were every bit as enfranchised by belief in Jesus as the rich. Writers of the period such as Tertullian, Clement of Alexandria, Origin, St. Jerome, and others who wrote in the second and third centuries argued that all work was honorable and so were all workingmen, and women, for housework, spinning, weaving, and cooking were viewed as honorable and desirable ways of living a righteous life. God himself worked to bring the world into being. Would he expect anything less from those he created?

Even the hermits and monks who renounced wealth took up work, on the other hand, with a passion. Among the early organizers—such as Saint Pachomius and Saint Anthony—of monastic life into communal and regulated living, as opposed to floating along in the remote deserts of Egypt or Syria as the early hermits did, work was both necessary and almost sacramental. *All* monks were assigned tasks and work, working as husbandmen, gardeners, smiths, bakers, weavers, fullers, tailors, carpenters, shoemakers, and copyists, for example.[72] Work was valuable for its own sake, as well as for the community. There was both a spiritual and material dimension to work that marked the intimate nexus between work and Christian living. They were not, literally, one in the same, but they were inseparable. To be a Christian was to embrace work. To work was to live the righteous Christian life, or, quite simply, to be right with God. Manual labor was lifted up as fostering the development of the virtues of charity, humility, and patience, all associated with the preaching of both Jesus and his early followers such as Paul.[73]

St. Augustine, who so influenced the formation of the church, also, of course, addressed work. And, again as usual, Augustine viewed work, as in virtually the entire world he encountered, both material and spiritual, in terms of his faith as a Christian.

What did work exist for but to exalt God? He wrote in perhaps his most famous work, *The City of God*, about work in almost panegyric terms, lyrical and sometimes rising to the level of poetry.

Work was not simply a physical interaction with the material world but an act rising to the spiritual level. And, recall, as you read Augustine below that this was written in the fourth century, long before the commercial and industrial revolutions transformed the world, before modern medicine, before the modern engines of war.

> "Has not the genius of man invented and applied countless astonishing arts [or skills], partly the result of necessity, partly the result

72. Ibid., 188.
73. Ibid., 188–89.

of exuberant invention, so that this vigor of mind, which is so active in the discovery not merely of superfluous but even of dangerous and destructive things, betokens an inexhaustible wealth in the nature which can invent, learn, or employ such arts?"[74]

"What wonderful—one might say stupefying—advances has human industry made in the arts of weaving and building, of agriculture and navigation!"

"With what endless variety are designs in pottery, painting, and sculpture produced, and with what skill executed!"

"What wonderful spectacles are exhibited in the theatres, which those who have not seen them cannot credit!"

"How skillful the contrivances for catching, killing, or taming wild beasts!"

"And for the injury of men, also, how many kinds of poisons, weapons, engines of destruction, have been invented, while for the preservation or restoration of health the appliances and remedies are infinite!"

"To express and gain entrance for thoughts, what a multitude and variety of signs there are, among which speaking and writing hold the first place!"

"What ornaments has eloquence at command to delight the mind! What wealth of song is there to captivate the ear! How many musical instruments and strains of harmony have been devised! What skill has been attained in measures and numbers! With what sagacity have the movements and connections of the stars been discovered!"[75]

Reading Augustine a thousand years before the Renaissance is like reading the prophets of the Old Testament looking forward to the coming of Jesus Christ. As Applebaum noted, "there is . . . something about the quoted passage, suggesting Augustine's view of human power over nature and human progress through technology, the arts, medicine, agriculture, and industry."[76]

---

74. Augustine, "Of the Blessings with Which the Creator Has Filled This Life, Obnoxious Though it Be to the Curse," in book 22, chapter 24 of *The City of God* (http://www.newadvent.org/fathers/120122.htm).

75. Ibid.

76. Applebaum, *The Concept of Work*, 191.

Augustine, in producing his version of a well-ordered monastic life, elaborated and explained certain areas. Some, like the handicapped, the old and the sick, were exempt from work. Manual labor was closely tied to the life of the mind, and the mind was to direct man to the contemplation and worship of God.

"Every workman," Applebaum wrote as he interpreted Augustine, "is instructed to work with an eye to serving God rather than Mammon, to work with confidence in God's solicitude for him, to remember that the fruits of labor are evidence of divine governance."[77] The Puritans no doubt saw this expression of God's providence, as confirming, at least in part, God's possible salvation. God blessed the work of the godly, remembering that this was not to lift them up higher than others with riches, but to share with those less blessed, the poor and the needy.

Before moving on to a closer scrutiny of the monastic movement and work, let's recapitulate a bit on the Greek and Roman views of work as opposed to those introduced by Judaism and Christianity, for there is a difference. Even though all agreed that agriculture was the noblest form of work, as the world became more complex over time, so did the attitudes.

Greeks and Romans tended to view manual labor as less edifying and ignoble—the work of slaves and the poor—than the life of the mind, typically that of philosophers and politicians. On the other hand, with the coming of Christianity, much of these attitudes changed. And one can easily note that some of this powerful Christian commitment to the poor was a legacy and continuation of a major theme in Judaism.

All Christians were regarded as brothers in Christ.[78] This spiritual equality was projected onto life on earth, and so while there still existed the obvious cultural distinctions between rich and poor, slave and free, and men and women, the Apostle Paul wrote that all are one in Christ Jesus.

It was, in many ways, an amazing transition from the stratified, hierarchical customs of the ancients, with emperors and slaves at the ends of the spectrum. In Christianity, masters and slaves were considered spiritual equals once they both accepted the Lordship of Jesus Christ. And those born to the lower social and economic classes—such as fishermen—could transcend their births and backgrounds. Some of these fishermen, like Peter, rose to be leaders in the early church, all based on their commitment

---

77. Ibid.

78. "There is neither Jew nor Gentile, neither slave nor free, nor is there male and female, for you are all one in Christ Jesus" (Gal 3:28).

and relationship to Christ, not their backgrounds, their wealth (or poverty), their education, titles, or any other human criteria. Furthermore, Christians were enjoined to take care of the poor, the widows, the lowly, the orphans and the destitute of society in general. Much of this commitment and philosophy was inherited from Judaism, but given fresh vigor and power by the teachings of Jesus.

Indeed, the Jewish God was a god who worked. After all, he created the world in six days, he considered idleness a sin, and he favored those who worked and even grew prosperous, always as long as they acknowledged the source of their wealth.

There arose within the Christian church in the first five or six centuries of its existence a movement—monasticism—which we have already seen not only called for all to work, but viewed work as beneficial to the spirit and soul of that individual. At the heart of the monastic movement were three rules: celibacy, poverty, and obedience. It was clearly enunciated and understood by all the foundational figures of monasticism—Saint Benedict of Nursia, St. Augustine, and others—that work was the enemy of idleness, which itself was a tool of the devil.

While prayer and medication and reading were the principal tasks, or work we can say, of the monks, they needed to be in the shop, in the fields, teaching in the schools, to advance their cause among the Christian public. That they did their work with thoroughness, keenness, and religious fervor also encouraged innovation in the workplace, such as in improving artificial irrigation with new windmills, watermills, and canals, for they were working not for themselves, but for God.

Curiously, some have linked the emergence of modern Western technology to the monks' way of life, as one student of phenomenon noted.[79] "It is one of the most amazing facts of Western cultural history," noted Ernst Benz, "that the striking acceleration and intensification of technological development in post-Carolingian Europe emanated from contemplative monasticism, such as the order of the Benedictines and its later reform orders, the Cluniacs and the Cistercians."[80]

Benz reminds us that under the influence of the Benedictine monks of the tenth century, the yield of agriculture in Central Europe was tripled, advancing under improved technologies. They were working for God, and the

---

79. Applebaum, *The Concept of Work*, 196, quoting from Ernst Benz's *Evolution and Christian Hope: Man's Concept of the Future from the Early Fathers to Teilhard de Chardin.*

80. Ibid.

Benedictine God was most certainly a worker who esteemed good work. God not only brought the universe into existence in six days of work, but he also was described as a potter and master builder. Indeed, in the first three books of the Bible, God's instructions for the building of the ark of the covenant, the tabernacle, and other instructions on sacrifices, laws, and customs are almost excruciating in their detail.[81]

Linking Christianity "with technology, and later of technology with progress," was given added fuel by the rise of Protestantism which looked to the creation of wealth and riches by work in God's will as a positive indicator of one's salvation.[82]

The very concept of progress, of a society moving forward to a particular end in time, was part of the Christian message. Christ will return, sometime in the future, and Christians are to be in constant preparation for that moment when Christ returns to claim his own. How and when this will happen is subject to much interpretation of Scripture (especially in the books of prophecy like Daniel and Revelations and portions of the Gospel, like Matthew, etc.) and beyond the scope of this little book. What is interesting is Benz's proposition that there is a reflection in the natural world of the concept of progress toward an end—eschatology, or the second coming of Christ—in the spiritual world. As man perfects himself in the image of God—a constant struggle both as individuals and collectively as God's people—and moves forward or, in worldly terms, makes progress over time to the second coming, so man does the same thing in the natural world. He progressively improves technology, always building on past efforts and improving them, over hundreds and thousands of years, a pale yet nonetheless recognizable mirroring of his spiritual progress, or lack of, as the case may be.

As noted, Christians hold to the concept that we are moving forward, making progress through time. This is unlike, let's say, a cyclical view of history, where history repeats itself, occurring in cycles that are easily recognizable: e.g., catastrophic wars, epidemics, etc. The principle of reincarnation subscribes to this theory. Everyone will return in some higher or lower form, depending upon circumstances described and understood within certain religious traditions, like Hinduism.

Benz's theory is that knowledge and wisdom in art, philosophy, and religion "is forgotten again and again. It is different with technology.

---

81. Ibid., 196–98. Following Applebaum's summary of main points made by Benz.
82. Ibid.

Inventions remain and spread until they are replaced by better ones." [83]
Presto, we have progress, each new age improving on the technology of the
last age, even with catastrophic reverses, wars, etc. that do not significantly
impede the evolution of progress in technology. And Christianity, with its
own built-in bias towards progress in the spiritual world, directly supports
what is, after all, a similar view of the world, technologically speaking.

Christians, from the time of the hard-working and inventive Benedictines of the tenth century and earlier, and, obviously, as we study the
explosion of new technologies in the past two centuries since then, have
always subscribed to the concept that we have a "working" God, one who
rewards work and punishes the idle and the lazy. He is also a God who calls
us to a vocation, as a little card that I have carried—and duplicated and
shared with many over the years—says so well.

> A vocation is a call from God,
> Urging you to be more than you are.
> God inspires everyone to think more,
> Pray more, and do more,
> In order to be more.
> The response is yours.[84]

Monasticism obviously emphasized the close relationship in Christian
life between the discipline of work and spiritual growth. While the various
orders—Benedictines, Augustinians, Cistercians, and Franciscans and Dominicans added in the thirteenth century—sometimes split hairs over the
exact placement of work in the hierarchy of their lives governed by prayer
and meditation, all agreed that the spiritual life was enhanced by work in
three ways: work helped overcome the danger of idleness; work created the
wherewithal for charity and doing good, as well providing for the monasteries; work was a way of exercising stewardship over nature.[85]

One of the most fascinating, and instructive, tracts from the medieval
period was written by a master craftsman, Theophilus, in a book entitled
De Diversis Artibus.[86] It is immensely useful for the view or attitudes towards work from a worker himself, but an immensely skilled one.

83. Ibid., 197.

84. Given to me by, I believe, a Maryknoll missionary in 1979 or 1980 while I was
living in New York City and working on a couple of books.

85. Applebaum, *The Concept of Work*, 237; quoting George Ovitt Jr. "Early Christian
Attitudes toward Manual Labor."

86. Dodwell, *Introduction to Theophilus*, 171ff.

Theophilus was probably a German, from northwestern Germany, and he wrote *De Diversis* probably between 1110 and 1140, perhaps more exactly in 1122–23. His treatise is divided into three books, one dealing with painting, the second with glass, and the third with metalwork. Theophilus also describes the carving of bone and the working of precious stones as well as creating ecclesiastical vessels "such as the chalice and censer; and fashioning musical instruments for the church, such as the bell and organ."[87]

Theophilus was undoubtedly a devout Christian, as well as master craftsman, since "his fundamental attitude toward work was that it was pursued, not for profit, but for the glory of God and for the perfection of self."[88]

George Ovitt cites the "seven-fold spirit" of work which Theophilus wrote for the preface of his third book. It is an extraordinary statement of basic theology with respect to Christianity and work, and worth savoring in full.

> Through the spirit of wisdom, you know that all created things proceed from God, and without Him nothing is.
>
> Through the spirit of understanding, you have received the capacity for skill—the order, variety, and measure with which to pursue your varied work.
>
> Through the spirit of counsel, you do not bury your talent given you by God, but, by openly working and teaching in all humility, you display it faithfully to all wishing to understand.
>
> Through the spirit of fortitude, you drive away all torpor of sloth, and whatever you assay [type in text; should be "essay," I think] with energy you bring with full vigour to completion.
>
> Through the spirit of knowledge accorded you, you are, in the abundance of your heart, the master of your skill and, with the confidence of a full mind, employ the abundance for the public good.
>
> Through the spirit of godliness, you regulate with pious care the nature, the purpose, the time, measure and method of the work and the amount of the reward lest the vice of avarice of [looks like another typo; should probably be "or"] cupidity steal in.
>
> Through the spirit of fear of the Lord, you remember that you can do nothing of yourself; you reflect that you have or intend nothing,

87. Applebaum, *The Concept of Work*, 238–39.

88. Ibid, 239, following George Ovitt Jr., *The Restoration of Perfection, Labor and Technology in Medieval Culture.*

unless accorded by God, but by believing, by acknowledging and rendering thanks, you ascribe to the divine compassion whatever you know, or are, or are able to do.[89]

The spiritual goal of moving closer to Christ through work comes through like a siren in the night in Theophilus's seven reminders of what work and life is all about. Work is not about satisfying self, but about satisfying God. And, not incidentally, God provides for man's ultimate satisfaction and pleasure with work well done. In other words, and here is a key element we have underscored throughout this little book, work is not just "work" and a job and a way to fulfill God's will, but it is satisfying and gratifying and, if done well and with the ultimate giver of all things in mind, a wonderful vocation given to men by God.[90]

During the terrible Depression of the 1930s when unemployment rose to unimaginable percentages of the work force, and men could not find work and had to line up to receive soup and shelter, and could not provide for themselves, and even less for their families, many turned desperate and despondent, and not a few committed suicide. Work, in this context, was almost as important for life as something elemental like food and water.

We jumped ahead a bit from Theophilus in the twelfth century to the Depression in the twentieth century. Work, however, is beginning to come alive as not just a "fact" of life, but, in the Christian context, a necessary and noble calling by God to do what you do, and do it well, from the simple farmers on the estates of the Roman empire to the sophisticated craftsmen of the medieval ages and on into "modern" times, usually conceived of by historians as beginning roughly in the fifteenth and especially in the sixteenth and seventeenth centuries.

In the mid-twentieth century a school of French historians developed a framework for looking at history, the *longue durée*, or the "long view" of history. Let's borrow from their model a bit. And let's put "work" as one of the "structures" of society.

We started out this chapter with the title of "How Work Got to Be a Dirty Word," and by that we mean that as societies and cultures became more complex, some work was considered noble and useful, while other

89. Applebaum, *The Concept of Work*, 239–41.

90. Or ibid., 264, quoting Ovitt, wrote: "In a way, Piers Plowman [a fourteenth century poem to work, truth, and love] is a fourteenth century expression of the medieval ideas identified by Ovitt, of seeing work *as a means of individual and communal spiritual perfection, rather than a means for personal gain*" [italics added].

work was considered base and servile. The former lifted and edified the nation and people—high government, art, philosophy, war—while the latter was simply necessary to support the former.

This is not the way that the God of the Hebrews viewed work, as we have seen. But as we moved past the Greeks into the Roman Empire and then into the medieval ages, work tended to be put a scale of values, from the noblest to the basest, which, of course, was the work done by slaves.

The introduction of Christianity challenged this view of work. Again, as we have considered, Christians of the first two or three centuries viewed all as equal before God—Jews, Gentiles, men, women, and even slaves if we extend the lasso a bit—and this was generally interpreted as not simply a spiritual equality before God, but also an equality right here on earth, or the "natural" world as some chose to refer to life in the here and now, in the physical world we inhabit, not our spiritual lives.

Gradually over the next thousand years, or from roughly the fourth or fifth centuries to the fifteenth or sixteenth—largely known as the "Middle Ages," an artificial construct by, again, French historians to describe the time between the end of the Roman Empire and the beginning of the "modern" age—Christians too slipped into the habit of separating the different categories of work. In the grossest sense, Christian people were separated into different classes, types, categories, or estates (the language of the historians), and each was assigned a different value in the world. At the top of the pyramid were of course emperors, kings, and popes, and at the bottom, occupying the widest part of the pyramid of importance, were those born to labor and work all their lives, in relatively servile occupations. And the work they performed at the bottom of the pyramid was not thought in any other terms than pedestrian and necessary, but certainly not noble or edifying, the stuff of peons and peasants and slaves.

But in this dismal picture of medieval society, there also arose the monastic movement, again, which we have considered above. It valued the work of all who joined, and work was considered not just necessary to sustain life, but to edify God.

And the concomitant of work in this book, or wealth, also was endowed with radically different evaluations. To some, especially the nobility, higher clergy, and emerging commercial classes, wealth was a privilege they enjoyed because of their birth, their calling, or the providence of God that distinguished them from all the others. But wealth, especially to devout Christians like Francis of Assisi—also of the twelfth century—was pushed aside as an impediment to one's walk with God. Francis, the founder of the Franciscan monastic order, embraced poverty with a passion, as did other monastic orders, although not as rigidly as the first Franciscans who emulated their founder in as much as was humanly possible. And if it wasn't humanly possible, then they turned to God to sustain and hold them up in their profession as they fasted, prayed, meditated, and embraced both poverty and celibacy. The stark contrast between the mighty Christian warriors who led the crusaders into the Holy Land with fire and sword, and the humble, barefoot, begging Franciscans is almost too much to encompass for anyone trying to describe the "nature" of Christianity in the Middle Ages. So, it is with little surprise that attitudes towards work and wealth also spanned the spectrum of the human experience.

If anything, society and culture has become immensely more complicated since the sixteenth century. But, for the sake of our conversation with Scripture and what it has to say about work and wealth, Scripture remains the same. It is unchanging. So as we move this consideration forward, we will have to come to grips with the historical reality that it is man who has changed rapidly from the end of the Middle Ages to today (however we characterize our age), not Scripture. The way of life today, so complex and multifaceted, has had to accommodate to Scripture, not the other way around. And it is with this consideration that we move along.

One of giants along this path of Christian history was Martin Luther, the German theologian monk who set off the firestorm of the Reformation in 1517. Borrowing from an oft-quoted book by Adriano Tigher, Applebaum summarized Luther's attitudes towards work. "For Luther, as it was for medieval thinkers and monastic thinkers, work was both a form of penance, a basis for charity and a defense against idleness."[91] "However," Applebaum observed, again, following Tigher, "Luther broke with monastic thinking [and Luther was himself an Augustinian monk] and the contemplative way of life. He considered that way of life to be selfishness on the part of the monks and an abdication of responsibility to the world at large. Thus, Luther's idea of work resulted in a universal extension, so that work became the universal base of society and the real cause of differing social classes."[92]

I'm not quite sure if work, as interpreted by Tigher and Applebaum, caused the rise of differing social classes, but, more important, Luther's

---

91. Applebaum, *The Concept of Work*, 321, quoting from Adriano Tigher, *Work [and] What It Has Meant to Men through the Ages*.

92. Ibid.

contribution to the reformation of the church was not so much a radical departure from the norm or accepted wisdom, but it was a *rediscovery* of principles and doctrine that had been in place since the beginnings of Christianity.

According to Applebaum, Luther condemned commerce as not real work, and he condemned profit for good measure "believing that the purpose of work was maintenance and nothing more." This was thoroughly in keeping with medieval Catholic teaching.

But, and it is a big "but," Luther was also strikingly original, in promoting the idea "that one best serves God by doing most perfectly the work of one's trade or profession." This seems innocuous enough and not particularly innovative. But Applebaum observes that "with this idea, Luther swept away the concept that there was a distinction between spiritual work and secular work—a belief which was prevalent in the Middle Ages . . . These concepts stressed the higher value of spiritual and contemplative work, and the necessity for the lower and less esteemed orders to work for the benefit of the higher orders, nobles, and clerics who were to have leisure to pursue the contemplative and spiritual life."[93]

I read this as a radical—but not unprecedented—renewal of the equality of all believers, and so, by extension, the equality of their work before God. If all men (and we are not going to be politically correct here; you know I mean women and children also) were equal before God as Paul expressed in his letter to the Galatians, "There is neither Jew nor Gentile, neither slave nor free, nor is there male and female, for you are all one in Christ Jesus," then all their work, all their offerings, all their prayers, all their lives—rich or poor, powerful or slaves—were equally valid.[94] The Middle Ages had, in fact, muddled this understanding of work within the true Christian context, but for that to happen two things have to occur: man gets involved in determining the meaning of Scripture; and, two, societies and cultures become more complex, more diversified and so force men to interpret Scripture more and more in keeping with "new" realities.

The first—men interpreting Scripture—is of course mandatory if one is a practicing Christian. Every new generation has to read Scripture for themselves and determine what it means. Did Jesus really mean to love your neighbor, for example? What if he is a scheming, mean-spirited, nonbeliever who reviles Christians? Do we really have to turn the other cheek and accept the slaps and insults?

93. All preceding quotes from ibid., 321–22.
94. Gal 3:28.

Let me suggest a few other quick examples to make the point. While slavery existed as an institution in the Bible, by the twentieth century slavery had all but been extinguished in most of (but not all) the world as a valid, legal institution. How do we reconcile the existence of an institution in Scripture that most of the modern world has determined was basically an evil?

What about obeying lawful authorities? In Romans 13:1–7 Paul admonishes us to obey the lawful governing authorities. We won't follow this fascinating thread since it takes us far afield of the subjects of work and wealth into obedience and authority (for another book!). Do we owe a monstrous governing authority such as Adolph Hitler's Third Reich obedience? The answer to this conundrum, by the way, is in Acts 5:27–29. The answer given by the judges at the Nuremberg Trials for war prisoners following the Second World War was that, "no, you do not have to obey authorities who violate the natural human rights inherent in all men."

My point is that while Scripture does not change, the habits, customs, and men's concepts of right and wrong *do* change over time. What is incumbent upon us is to determine—in the midst of all these changes in the "modern" world, for example—what both the word and spirit of Scripture call us to believe and do, or, in the case of this little book, how to handle the subjects of work and wealth.

Returning to our theme, since the Middle Ages—omitting for the most part the religious orders who marched to their own drummers of obedience, celibacy, and poverty—had stretched the work that Christians do into such a distortion of—let's call it—the equality principle invoked by Paul, how did Reformation activists such as Luther bring Christian behavior back in line with Scripture?

Luther combined all work, "the work of clerics . . . and the work of everyday tradesmen, craftsmen, and peasants" into the only category that existed, God's work. The cleric's work—prayer, fasting, preaching, etc.—was no higher on the pecking order than the work of the cobbler.[95] This was a very egalitarian point of view which got Luther in some trouble, but that for another study of Luther and the peasants' rebellion of the mid-1520s.

In Luther's determination, all must work at what God calls us to do, and so work becomes a part of one's calling, and there was nothing more sacred than following the call to obey God.

95. Applebaum, *The Concept of Work*, 323.

Luther broke free from the notion that work for most of us was just a joyless fulfilling of our calling, simply a way of sustaining life and obeying Scripture.

"Your work is a very sacred matter," Luther wrote while commenting on Psalms 128:2.

> God *delights* [emphasis added] in it, and through it wants to bestow His blessing on you. This praise of work should be inscribed on all tools, on the forehead and face that sweat from toiling ["You will eat the fruit of your labor; blessings and prosperity will be yours."] . . . the pious, who fear the Lord, labor with a ready and cheerful heart; for they know God's command and will. Thus a pious farmer sees this verse written on his wagon, and plow, a cobbler sees it on his leather and awl, a laborer sees it on wood and iron.[96]

And, I might add, a writer will see it printed, and, finally, published, the fruit of his labors, God working through my mind, heart, and fingers tapping away on the keyboard.

If Luther championed the equality of all work before God, that work was part of one's calling, and no one class or category of person had a higher calling than any other, one of Luther's contemporaries on the Protestant Reformation, John Calvin, was not quite so egalitarian in his assessment of work. It was part of one's calling, yes, but it did not imply one simply worked at what one's father did or what life threw at you. God's providence also gifted one with the ability to rise out of his circumstances, change his life for better, improve yourself and the world you were born into by dint of hard work, imagination, and knowing that God rewarded those who availed themselves of the liberty and freedom to raise themselves up.

As we have developed in an earlier chapter, Calvin and the Puritans who sprang from Calvin's theology gave rise to the Protestant work ethic, that work was a force that could earn salvation, or, at the very least, be a strong indicator of God's favor, and so be understood as a confirmation of salvation.

Tigher commented that a new attitude toward labor and work was championed by Calvin.[97] Calvin, in some ways, departed from the past more than Luther, who rediscovered the principles of the Reformation in the original Scriptures, and, in reaffirming them—such as the primacy of faith over works as the road to salvation—kicked off the Reformation.

---

96. Ibid., 323, quoting from Ewald Plass, ed., *What Luther Says.*

97. Ibid., 325.

At the heart of the Protestant work ethic, well developed by Weber as we have seen above, was the "teaching that it is one's duty to extract the greatest possible gain from work."[98] And, "success, which is proven by profit, is the certain indication that the chosen profession is pleasing to God . . . Puritanism . . . endorses and permits the effort to become wealthy," and so "wealth is reconciled with a good conscience."[99] Or, put another way, "good works were not a way of attaining salvation, but they were indispensable as proof that salvation had been attained."[100] This is dynamite in the hands of all Christians seeking to find the meaning of work, and the means to salvation.

Work could produce wealth, but wealth alone was not the road to salvation. It could, in fact be a great impediment as we have seen in other parts of this book. But Calvin lived in new times, marked by the rise of trade, the commercial classes, early industries, a time when mobility and enterprise and new wealth began to replace a static and immobile society and culture. New ways had to be found to accommodate Scripture—and we are largely limiting ourselves to work and wealth, but other elements were obviously involved—to the new times. This was Calvin's genius. He didn't compromise Scripture, but he adapted the rise of the commercial revolution to conform to scriptural principles.[101]

As one of the great historians of the past, Richard Tawney, commented, "Calvin did for the bourgeoisie of the sixteenth century what Marx did for the proletariat of the nineteenth."[102] They both—Calvin and Marx—produced ideologies to match the economic realities of the time.

At this point, we break off before going to the "modern" period in the last chapter and how it has envisioned work and its articulation with Scripture. Applebaum helps us set up the transition from Calvinism to more unbridled capitalism.

"It is important," Applebaum observes,

> to distinguish Calvinism—which combined an ascetic vocational
> ethic with the exaltation of work, and which put certain restraints

98. Ibid.

99. Ibid.

100. Ibid., 325.

101. Close students of the Bible will of course recognize we are writing here generally of the "cultural captivity" of the Bible, but we are trying to keep this approach to work and wealth in Scripture as free of epistemological and theological terms as possible.

102. Applebaum, *The Concept of Work*, 326, following R. H. Tawney, *Religion and the Rise of Capitalism*.

on capital wealth—from that of the modern concept of capitalism, with its hedonism, severe competition, extreme specialization, feverish labor, and vocational humanism. All this belongs to a later period—to the period of Adam Smith at the end of the eighteenth century and does not fit the earlier forms of the bourgeois spirit as mixed with religion, which advocated frugality, and modesty, and sought economic advantage in the light of God's community. Troelsch (1981, 647) comments that it is the ethics of Benjamin Franklin rather than those of Jeremy Bentham and Adam Smith.[103]

As related by historians and theologians, the relationship of work with capital was the nicer brand of capitalism. It was not necessarily invented by Calvin, but it was given a great push due to his importance in launching the Reformation and being, essentially, the spiritual inspiration and practical source of the Puritans, or, of course, Calvinism itself.

Work was a part of life, Calvin agreed wholeheartedly. Combined with work it was a form of asceticism, especially when it came to what to do with the profits generated by work within the growing world of capitalism. To summarize Calvin's views on work and wealth would take another few volumes. But, essentially, he looked upon work and wealth as something God-given that came with certain responsibilities.

Applebaum, following Troelsch, does a good job of summarizing this critical aspect of Calvin's views on work and wealth. "Calvinism stressed work as asceticism, and profit as a sign of the blessings of God. But profit was not to exceed certain limits." And here's where it gets very instructive on how different Calvin and his followers viewed profits—and wealth— from work. "Work and profit were not intended for purely personal interest, with the entrepreneur seen as a steward of the gifts of God. He was to increase his capital and utilize it for the good of society as a whole, retaining for himself only that account which was necessary to provide for his own needs. All surplus wealth should be used for works of public utility and philanthropy,"[104] which of course sounds very familiar to the ancient Hebrew prescription on what to do with the wealth and surplus generated

---

103. Ibid., 327–28, drawing from Ernst Troeltsch, *The Social Teaching of the Christian Church*. And the reader might wish to zip back to an earlier chapter where we described the movie *Wall Street*, starring Michael Douglas, for the free-for-all expression of capitalism, ugly in the extreme, featuring unbridled greed.

104. Applebaum, *The Concept of Work*, 328.

by work.[105] It is not for you, but the usufruct is for all, not just for one individual, his family and friends.

"The Calvinist Church engaged in much charitable activity, giving loans to poor people without interest or requiring security," noted Applebaum. "Calvinism preached against usury and the exploitation of the poor. Christian Social elements are part of Calvinism, and even a form of Christian socialism."[106]

At the core of Calvinism was always the rule or principle that "the person who achieved success in business and in is calling was probably destined for salvation," with the emphasis on "probably."[107] People were expected to make "a success of their lives on their own and through frugality, hard work, energy, and foresight." And as Applebaum summarized the Calvinist/Puritan influence on attitudes towards work within Christendom, "such is the legacy of Puritanism in England, and such is the legacy which found such a favorable reception and environment in the United States, a young nation of opportunity which provided so many outlets for the man of action, for the individualist, and for the man willing to work hard and make a success of himself. Indeed, the mythology of America, as represented in the life of Benjamin Franklin, is seen as one big success story, based on hard work, frugality, and old-fashioned morality."[108]

This is so at odds with prevailing attitudes toward work in the second decade of the twenty-first century as to appear we are considering two different universes entirely: and perhaps we are. Applebaum points to leaders such as Franklin D. Roosevelt and Martin Luther King Jr. as a new breed of more caring individuals "who stressed community and the communal path to salvation."[109] In fact, if one turns to the book of Acts, especially chapters 2–5, Christians shared much of what they had, but as very good article on the web illustrates, not by force or coercion but voluntarily.[110] We can conclude that Christians have always struggled with the appropriate way to

---

105. See chapter above where a section on ancient Hebrew attitudes towards work and the distribution of one's wealth and/or surplus is dealt with, or Tzedakah. See also my column on Maimonides, Clayton, "Religions."

106. Applebaum, *The Concept of Work*, 328, following Troeltsch.

107. Ibid.

108. Ibid.

109. Ibid.

110. Lindsley, "Does the Book of Acts Command Socialism?" And the answer, for those interested in the short version, is "no."

handle their wealth, as individuals or as community, or something flexible and in between.

Let's pretend we're biblical scholars and plunge ahead a bit here in time, leaving Calvin and Puritans for the moment back in the sixteenth and seventeenth centuries. Let's do, in fact, what the prophets of old did, see into the future, except we have an advantage, the future from the seventeenth century forward were centuries we have already lived.

In the seventeenth and eighteenth centuries the acquisition of new wealth through the evolving system of capitalism caused many to pause: how was all this lining up with what Scripture had to say about wealth and work? From the steam locomotives and railroad tracks of the early nineteenth century to rocket shots into space in the twenty-first century, the panorama of the human experience vastly changed.

Indeed, the rapid increase in wealth of a relatively few in society, with the concomitant increase in the many laboring in the mines, the mills, and the workshops of the industrial revolution led in part to the rise of radical socialism, or Marxism, as formally posited by Karl Marx as we have seen above. But what was true for a grimy and sooty London or Manchester being transformed by the industrial revolution was not necessarily true for pioneer farmers and ranchers moving across the Appalachians and into the central and western parts of the United States. Capitalism began to take on my different shadings, and so the stability of Scripture became even more important.

Perhaps no one represented best the Enlightenment age's attitude towards work than Benjamin Franklin. In his *Poor Richard's Almanac* he extolled the virtues of work and thrift. A Deist Franklin may have been, but he knew his Bible and Scripture, and one can sense the teachings on work and wealth seeping into Franklin in his paeans to the work ethic.

Adam Smith, a Scottish contemporary of Franklin's, produced in his 1776 *Wealth of Nations* the classic study that underlays the modern study of economics. What he is probably best known for is the self-interest principle: a society is best organized and progresses when the self-interest of the individual is given free reign, and when government keeps its hands out of the business of the nation's economics. In other words, as the world became increasingly complex, added new forms of wealth-making, and moved into industrialization, capital expanded dramatically, and there was an even greater gulf between the "common working man" and the merchants and industrialists amassing great fortunes. Someone had to explain why it was working the way it did, and what were its strengths and weaknesses. Smith did that for economics.

In the nineteenth century and continuing into the twentieth, it had become evident that "the calculating ethos of profit and loss was rapidly replacing the traditional, religious principles of community, family and individuals as ends in themselves."[111] It became evident to Karl Marx and others that "labor" was no longer an individual, but had to be treated in the same category as "capital," in the sterilized equations that explained the world now being reorganized under capitalism. We need not get lost in the multiple threads of economic history, other than to observe—still keeping our eyes focused on work and wealth in Scripture—that the individual and his relationship to his God, to Jesus Christ, was being lost in equations which explained how capitalism worked. There was labor, there was capital, there was surplus value, there were all sorts of ingredients, but the connection between the poor slob working in a textile mill in Manchester, England, or Lyons, France, or in the iron and steel mills of Pittsburgh, Pennsylvania, and what his Bible had to instruct him on work and wealth was generally eroded, even though the nineteenth century continued to be the "century when the ideology of the work ethic was fostered by religious, social, and political leader, as well as the leader of industry and commerce."[112] As Hannah Arendt saw it in the mid-twentieth century, there were huge "contradictions between work as a creative and satisfying process [and so, following the script set out in the Old Testament], and labor which was nothing more than an instrumental activity," by which the author presumably meant labor was an impersonal factor in an economic equation.[113]

Arendt defined quite well the modern challenge. Work as described in Scripture, written more than 2000 years ago, has changed radically in today's twenty-first-century world, and presumably will be altered just as radically in the next 2000 years. The challenge then becomes, how to adapt our world—thinking always of work and wealth for the moment—to Scripture, not, by the way, the other way around, adapting Scripture to the ways of life—culture, morals, economics, etc.—prevailing at the time. That phenomenon is called the "cultural captivity" of the Bible.

We as individuals change over time. And our culture and civilization changes over time as well.

111. Applebaum, *The Concept of Work*, 584.
112. Ibid., 585.
113. Ibid., 585–86.

What concerned people in this country in 1765 was different from 1865 (try the end of the Civil War), and 1965 for example, when women's liberation, the Civil Rights movement, and the Vietnam War were all demanding our attention. I can envision a sermon preached then on how bra burning was against Scripture, or how the very same act confirmed that Jesus really liked women and wanted them to be free.

As the Civil War drew to a close, for example, a hot issue among Southerners was "why did we lose, and so catastrophically at that?" Whose side was God on in this immense internecine conflict that still casts shadows on our world today?

Southerners turned to the Old Testament for answers, likening their defeat to the rebukes and corrections inflicted on the ancient Hebrews by God for their iniquities.

The North ascribed their victory to championing the end of slavery and freeing a people. A good sermon might have been entitled something like "He hath loosed the fateful lightning of His terrible swift sword," which is straight from the "Battle Hymn of the Republic" of course, and—like most of the rest of the "Battle Hymn"—from Scripture and especially the book of Revelation. The sermon might have played well in Gettysburg, Pennsylvania, but probably not in Richmond, Virginia.

Every age has to contend with the fact that while Scripture—on wealth and work for example—does not change, the customs, habits, and culture of a civilization do change. The tough question is how do we interpret Scripture when we have grown so complicated, so complex, and, apparently, so sophisticated, so modern, so scientific, so in-charge-of-it-all? Scripture seems, by contrast, static, antique, boring, and old fashioned, and not relevant at all to the world we live in. Roman yeomen farmers happily planting away in their vineyards in Tuscany are a far cry from a factory worker doing relatively mindless repetitive drone-like work day in and day out. I know even this is an old stereotype that belongs in the past when considering modern Western civilization, but in many parts of the world that stereotype is the reality. In the U.S., Europe, Japan and some other parts of the world, the worker may not be chained—figuratively if not literally—to her machine, but is more than likely glued to a computer screen, although this stereotype is too changing.[114]

114. Modern factories have initiated practices that give the worker—part of a team—in the manufacturing process a far different perspective of his worth and value in the production of automobiles. See, for example, Warner and Anderson, "Putting it On the Line," especially the subtopic, "Culture and Continuous Improvement."

As the world tries to adapt Scripture to fit its own needs, the results as we've noted above are what theologians and scholars call the "cultural captivity" of the Bible, or how we adopt biblical principles and rules and laws to our times. Or, put another way, each different culture—of let's say the Roman Empire, or medieval Europe, or of the Enlightenment—reads and interprets Scripture to suit its fashions.

That there is widespread dissatisfaction with work in industrial society is well documented in modern literature. That the modern situation should provoke such dissatisfaction and frustration should be no surprise to those who study the human condition, and, more intensely, the human condition with the Judeo-Christian tradition where work is so important in defining one's relationship to God and one's source of self-esteem.[115]

As Applebaum notes, "the basic dimension of work in the twentieth century [and one might add, continuing into the twenty-first century] is that it is seen as an instrumental activity, as a means for acquiring income for subsistence and consumption, and that there is little or no satisfaction or meaning to be found in the workplace."[116] But even these old stereotypes are slowly vanishing. While Applebaum does not specifically examine any one mass production assembly line (such as the Mercedes Benz plant in Tuscaloosa, Alabama, an ultramodern expression of the type), Applebaum does address the solutions arising to make work meaningful. "There are attempts," he concludes, "to introduce new methods in the factory, such as quality circles and autonomous work teams, to increase work satisfaction, along with productivity."[117]

At the core of the issue is, of course, finding meaning in work that is far removed, in time and space, from the time of the ancients when the agricultural cycle governed life and work. "Whether work has the same central meaning," Applebaum wrote, "to people's lives as in the past, it is, nevertheless, still true that work is probably the most important single factor in status and self-respect for the individual."[118] And that modern reflection is most assuredly sustained by our examination of work and wealth in Scripture in this book.

115. Applebaum, *The Concept of Work*, 586, citing Michael Burrawoy, *Manufacturing Consent*, E. J. Roethlisberger and W. J. Dickson, *Management and the Worker*, Studs Terkel, *Working*, and James O'Toole, *Work in America: Report of a Special Task Force to the Secretary of Health, Education and Welfare*.

116. Applebaum, *The Concept of Work*, 586.

117. Ibid.

118. Ibid.

One of the challenging phenomenon of the "modern" world, characterized by the immense transformations produced by the industrial and technical revolutions from the nineteenth century onwards, is releasing people from work into the slippery world of leisure. If most of the necessary work in the world of the twenty-first century can be produced by half as many workers due to economic efficiencies, scientific advancements, computers, robots, and other assorted wizardry, then what are people going to do? If work is still "necessary for their self-respect and their psychological well-being," and there *is* no work, where does one derive that self-respect so necessary to sustain life and sanity?

The answer has to come from somewhere other than men's imagination. It comes from Scripture, which has to unravel two threads: one, what did God rule or say on work and wealth? And, two, how successfully has man reflected those principles so that all men can be within God's will in a highly complicated world.

Questions for Discussion:

- How did work become such a "dirty" word?
- What does Scripture say about work?
- Why are some of the early Christian communities sometimes thought of as communal or even socialist in their patterns of wealth and its distribution?
- What was the "great reversal"?
- What problem did the rich young ruler have with Jesus' advice on what he needed to do to enter the kingdom of God?
- How did Christians begin to think of work "not simply a physical interaction with the material world, but an act rising to the spiritual level?"
- Why and how did the monastic movement begin?
- And what was the relationship of work and wealth within monasticism?
- How did Theophilus, the master craftsman of the twelfth century, think of work?
- What did Martin Luther do to the concept of work and calling?

- How did John Calvin and Calvinism in general tie together wealth and salvation?

- What is the "cultural captivity" of the Bible?

7

Some Very Hard Truths

As Jesus started on his way, a man ran up to him and fell on his knees before him. "Good teacher," he asked, "what must I do to inherit eternal life?"

"Why do you call me good?" Jesus answered. "No one is good—except God alone. You know the commandments: 'You shall not murder, you shall not commit adultery, you shall not steal, you shall not give false testimony, you shall not defraud, honor your father and mother.'"

"Teacher," he declared, "all these I have kept since I was a boy."

Jesus looked at him and loved him. "One thing you lack," he said. "Go, sell everything you have and give to the poor, and you will have treasure in heaven. Then come, follow me."

At this the man's face fell. He went away sad, because he had great wealth.

Jesus looked around and said to his disciples, "How hard it is for the rich to enter the kingdom of God!"

The disciples were amazed at his words. But Jesus said again, "Children, how hard it is to enter the kingdom of God! It is easier for a camel to go through the eye of a needle than for someone who is rich to enter the kingdom of God."[1]

THERE ARE NUMEROUS PLACES in the Bible where we read some hard truths about life and work and wealth that sound most unbiblical, most in tune with the world rather than the spiritual world which Jesus taught about as being of primary importance. Actually, he is the author of some of these harsh lessons.

1. Matt 10:17–24.

One of them is captured in the above story about the rich young man asking Jesus what he must do to inherit eternal life. We examine a parable along the same lines below, the parable of the talents. Neither takes long to read. Note that, for all of you—including yours truly—who tend to over-write and explain far more than any reader really needs to comprehend a central truth or message, it is nonetheless important to make the message as clear as possible.

Many of these truths and lessons are in the books of Proverbs and Ecclesiastes and they tell of life and its harsh realities in unvarnished terms. In other words, they tell it like it is in what many of us would describe as the "real world." They are like a bucket of cold water splashed in the face to wake us up to reality. *This* is what the real world is like, stupid. Stop trying to live like Jesus, or follow his teachings and instructions literally. It is impossible.[2] They are, as the title to this chapter implies, however, very harsh truths, but truths nonetheless.

Just a quick sampling is enough to convince anyone that the Bible is not just about angels flying around singing heavenly praises to the Lord and asking us to follow suit. It is about real people facing real issues, especially when faced with decisions to make on work and wealth.

"The rich rule over the poor, and the borrower is slave to the lender," observed the author of Proverbs, usually thought to be Solomon, the immensely wise king who followed his father David on the throne of Israel. He added this to give a softer context to the harsh realities governing rich and poor: the "rich and poor have this in common: The Lord is the Maker of them all."[3]

Not all tough reflections and observations are in the Old Testament. Jesus told a parable about the talents, and it is one of the hardest lessons in the Bible about work and wealth, especially the latter. Let's examine it, for we are in the truth business here. If you don't have your Bible handy, here is the parable in response to a question from his disciples on what the kingdom of heaven will be like.

This was not an uncommon question, by the way. Jesus heard it often, in different forms: what will the kingdom be like? How can I be saved for life eternal?

As you read the parable, be very aware that "talents" have two meanings, and both are equally applicable in the parable. One is a measure of weight, usually of gold or silver, and so it means coins in the ancient world.

2. But, of course, St. Francis of Assisi did just that.

3. Prov 7:22.

In the second meaning, talent means gifts or skills in English and other languages. You can derive the truest meaning of the parable if, as you read, you keep the second meaning—gifts, skills, as in those you use in your work, for example—in mind.

> For it [the Kingdom of God] will be like a man going on a journey, who called his servants and entrusted to them his property. To one he gave five talents, to another two, to another one, to each according to his ability. Then he went away. He who had received the five talents went at once and traded with them, and he made five talents more. So also he who had the two talents made two talents more. But he who had received the one talent went and dug in the ground and hid his master's money. Now after a long time the master of those servants came and settled accounts with them. And he who had received the five talents came forward, bringing five talents more, saying, "Master, you delivered to me five talents; here I have made five talents more." His master said to him, "Well done, good and faithful servant. You have been faithful over a little; I will set you over much. Enter into the joy of your master." And he also who had the two talents came forward, saying, "Master, you delivered to me two talents; here I have made two talents more." His master said to him, "Well done, good and faithful servant. You have been faithful over a little; I will set you over much. Enter into the joy of your master." He also who had received the one talent came forward, saying, "Master, I knew you to be a hard man, reaping where you did not sow, and gathering where you scattered no seed, so I was afraid, and I went and hid your talent in the ground. Here you have what is yours." But his master answered him, "You wicked and slothful servant! You knew that I reap where I have not sown and gather where I scattered no seed? Then you ought to have invested my money with the bankers, and at my coming I should have received what was my own with interest. So take the talent from him and give it to him who has the ten talents. For to everyone who has will more be given, and he will have an abundance. But from the one who has not, even what he has will be taken away. And cast the worthless servant into the outer darkness. In that place there will be weeping and gnashing of teeth" (Matt 25:14–30).

What is the meaning of this rather harsh parable that punishes the seemingly innocent soul who, fearing his master, simply squirreled away what he was given, and returned it?

At the heart of this message is that we all are endowed with talents—as in skills or gifts—and God expects us to do something with them, like work and multiply what you have, a form of stewardship that is part of the work and wealth message. We are all stewards of God's resources. We are not meant simply to sit on what we have been given—talent—but do something with it. The Puritans understood this principle well, and Max Weber described it with equal candor and clarity. He called it the Protestant work ethic that essentially drove capitalism. We don't have to buy into the entire argument, and people have been arguing over Weber's thesis ever since he published it more than a hundred years ago, but part of the work ethic is carried forward in this parable.

What stumps most people is that Jesus, in telling it, expected you to do some interpreting and thinking on your own. The master was not being mean or cruel or erratic by rewarding the servant with the five talents and sending the servant with the one talent spinning down into the dark. He told the parable precisely to make his point that we are *all* gifted by God, some to a greater degree than others, and God *expects* you use those gifts for the greater good of all, but, equally important, to fulfill your God-given role as worker, provider, protector, inventor, nurturer, and improver of your own world.

We are not to sit back and wait for God to gift us, to provide for us, to shower prosperity on us, to enjoy the usufruct of having chosen to follow Jesus. We are to be *active* not *passive* believers and actors.

So, with that as background, Hugh Whelchel, in his blog lesson on the talents, provided a nice explanation, summarized in five points. Remember, this is simply emphasizing part of the older message from the Old Testament, upgraded and given more immediacy in this parable.[4]

Welchel's "Five Lessons for Our Lives from the Parable of the Talents" has a particularly good analysis and we extract from it below.

Success is a product of our work. Or, no work, little or no success. The Puritans could be expected to applaud loudly this one. Ben Franklin too, and on down through the makers and shakers of the world today.

God always gives us everything we need to do what he has called us to do. God will provide once you discover the plan for your life.

We are not all created equal. In spite of the felicitous phrase incorporated into our Declaration of Independence by Thomas Jefferson, we are all different.[5]

We work for the Master, not for our own selfish purposes. This, of course, flies in the face of why many Americans work so hard, but it *is* one of those

4. Whelchel, "Five Lessons."
5. Clayton, "All Men Are Not Created Equal."

harsh truths the title to this chapter alludes to. When you give your life over to Christ, that's when the satisfaction begins to seep in and through you, not when you kick back and count your achievements, your property, your investments, what you have done to lift yourself up. You will never be satisfied with all the wealth. And you will worry the rest of your life if you will lose it.

We will be held accountable. This is perhaps the most important of the five lessons from this parable. Accountability is not a happy phrase. It implies that someone else will judge you, and, usually, that the standards will be pretty high. On the other hand, we have all the rules, we've been given the equipment, we've even got love and forgiveness built into the equation, and we have but to trust God. Don't bury your talent in the ground. Use it! If you fail now and then and fall down, pick yourself up, and always reach up for God's hand. It will *always* be there for you to take hold of. Yes, you will be held accountable, but only if you don't try.

Reality, of course, comes at us all the time, usually in the attempt to subvert our faith in God. And the Bible does not sugarcoat the world.

How about this one for a dash of reality? "The rich man's wealth is his strong city," or his protection against many troubles in life.[6]

John Winthrop and the Puritan divines would probably have agreed, but with a caveat or two, such the following: "Wealth is not an evil in itself. It has distinct advantages. On the other hand, "the ruin of the poor is their poverty."[7] Even Jesus spoke to the plight of the poor in a rather harsh fashion. "The poor you will always have with you. But you will not always have me."[8]

Edmund Morgan, in his biography of John Winthrop, wrote and quoted Winthrop on another of the great—and hard—truths in Scripture related to work and wealth. "Winthrop never lost an opportunity to affirm his belief that the powers that be were ordained of God and must be honored and respected accordingly. While still aboard the *Arbella*, he had reminded the other passengers that 'God Almightie in his most holy and wise providence hath soe disposed of the Conditcion of mankind, as in all times some must be rich some poore, some highe and eminent in power and dignitie; others meane and in subjeccion.'"[9]

---

6. Logos Bible Software, *Old Testament Survey Series: The Wisdom Literature and Psalms*, 2. "Regarding wealth," and other places within this excellent app on the Bible.

7. Ibid.

8. Matt 26:11.

9. Morgan, *The Puritan Dilemma*, 88.

There is no way to disguise the meaning of these truths of wealth, the rich, and the poor in both Old Testament and New Testament literature. Some will be rich, and some will be poor. We cannot nail down or perceive God's will exactly in all of this, simply because we are not God. It may sound harsh, unjust, unfair, and simply wrong for some to be rich and so many—usually—to be poor, but look around you, even in the godliest of people and society, and to deny this reality is simply to deny the truth.

And even when governments turn to socialism, or communism (simply another brand of socialism), and classes are eliminated, the rich chased out of the countries, or destroyed, and everyone leveled so there is no more poverty and all are equal, it doesn't work. There will always be the favored—such as the members of the party, the military, and others privileged in rigidly socialist states—and the rest of the people, if not desperately poor as in parts of Africa, or Asia, or even Latin America, poor by comparison to those favored and benefitting from the system.

And Scripture does not hide reality behind an artificial mask of all is well if one but believes. "The poor plead for mercy," the writer of Proverbs observed, "but the rich answer harshly."[10] "The wealth of the rich is their fortified city; they imagine it a wall too high to scale."[11] That line along could generate a commentary of many pages, but, in summary, the rich think they have it made, but nothing they hide or put behind a wall or shield (property, stock market, gold, etc.) is so safe not be vulnerable to loss and destruction. Proverbs 15:16 summarized it nicely: "Better is little with the fear of the Lord than great treasure and trouble therewith." Or Proverbs 23, verses 4 and 5: "Do not wear yourself out to get rich; do not trust your own cleverness. Cast but a glance at riches, and they are gone, for they will surely sprout wings and fly off to the sky like an eagle."

Ecclesiastes, a book of truth if there ever was one, hits the nail on the head with respect to wealth, and never having enough: "Whoever loves money never has enough; whoever loves wealth is never satisfied with their income."[12] Or, how about, "The sleep of a laborer is sweet, whether they eat little or much, but for the rich, their abundance permits them no sleep."[13]

The writer of Ecclesiastes, usually attributed to Solomon, spares nothing in his bare bones analysis of the realities of life. "I have seen a grievous evil under the sun: wealth hoarded to the harm of its owners, or wealth lost

10. Prov 18:23.

11. Prov 18:11.

12. Eccl 5:10.

13. Eccl 5:12

through some misfortune, so that when they have children there is nothing left for them to inherit. *Everyone comes naked from their mother's womb, and as everyone comes, so they depart* [emphasis added]. They take nothing from their toil that they can carry in their hands."[14]

This reminded me of an old story—probably apocryphal—of when billionaire Howard Hughes passed away.

Someone asked, "How much did he leave behind?"

The answer, by some wit, "All of it."

Another truth, with respect to wealth, comes to us—as noted above—from Proverbs: "Rich and poor have this in common: The Lord is the Maker of them all."[15] We simply have to trust in his wisdom on this one. You will rack your brain to a frazzle trying to figure out some mysteries in the world we inhabit, like why did the Lord make some rich and the rest poor? But, rest assured, he can bring the rich down as fast as they rose up, and the poor can get on God's elevator to the next floor of wealth just as easily as those coming down.

Proverbs also informs us of the transparently obvious in many cases: "The rich rule over the poor, and the borrower is slave to the lender." And as a long time mortgage holder and borrower, I say *Amen* to that. It is truth; it is a hard truth, but truth nonetheless, just as is the gentler verse 9: "The generous will themselves be blessed, for they share their food with the poor." With that verse, we move into answering the question, well what do we do with the wealth or resources we generate?

Hurting or not helping the poor was almost always considered a sin of omission among Hebrews and early Christians. Verse 16 comments that "one who oppresses the poor to increase his wealth and one who gives gifts to the rich—both come to poverty." James 2:15–17 is one of many who also addresses this issue: "Suppose a brother or a sister is without clothes and daily food. If one of you says to them, 'Go in peace; keep warm and well fed,' but does nothing about their physical needs, what good is it? In the same way, faith by itself, if it is not accompanied by action, is dead."[16]

With wealth, obviously, comes some accountability and responsibility, much of which flies in the face of the modern age's devotion to leisure and the pursuit of leisure. Here we move back into the field of work a bit, for in the modern workplace, one can accumulate goods and resources (wealth) and not have to work six days a week, ten hours a day, like was often the

14. Eccl 5:13–15.

15. Prov 22:2.

16. Jas 2:15–17.

lot of the worker in the past. One can work four days, six hours a day, often at home, sitting at ones computer, and generate plenty. The issue then becomes a somewhat hard one—as hinted in the title to this chapter—what to do with this wealth, other than spend it on oneself in pursuit of self-gratifying pleasure and leisure?

James, above, answers the question, but leaves the details to the occasion.

I have a problem that I face almost every day: phone or mail solicitations to help the needy, or those in need from their particular circumstances: the police in need of flak vests; retired firemen in need; legless veterans in need; children starving in [you can fill in the blank] need; the Salvation Army in need; the Red Cross in need; abandoned and starving pets in need—and the list goes on endlessly. What do I do? I'd like to help many of them, all of them actually, enfold them in an embrace of love and say, "here is a check, here is my credit card, here is my money, here I even volunteer my arm to the Red Cross, here is my blood."

But I can't do it all. Actually, I used to donate blood regularly but since going annually on mission trips to Honduras, the Red Cross figures I was in a "malarial" region and so my blood is tainted. Sigh, even doing good can be a problem.

Without getting too humorous here, the issue is what to do with what you make or inherit or gain in some other legal fashion. It is not a simple issue, for it is tied in with work. As we move further into the twenty-first century, those of us in the "developed" countries, largely in the northern hemisphere—North America, Europe, Japan, parts of Asia, etc.—are achieving more in our work, defined in multitudinous fashions, having more free or leisure time, and so what do we do with this surplus of wealth and time? Do you take the family on a cruise to the Bahamas, or perhaps give a dairy cow ($650) to a family in need? Keep reading.

The answer, if you have gotten this far, is pretty simple. Executing the answer, or putting it into action, is not always so simple. Give yourself and your wealth to God and let him distribute to those in need. And God is usually best, but not only, represented by the church.

As I write this I am reading a wonderful pamphlet put together by World Vision (for their Christmas 2013 campaign), devoted to helping the poor around the world. World Vision is "motivated by our faith in Jesus Christ, [and] we serve alongside the poor and oppressed as a demonstration of God's unconditional love for all people."[17] I have their pamphlet open

17. From World Vision web site: http://www.worldvision.org/about-us/who-we-are

to a page that advertises "Give a Goat, Save a child's life with milk, cheese and much more." Goats were available at the going rate of $75. Actually, I gave a goat in my brother's name for Christmas 2013.

Proverbs 28:27 sustains me in my goat giving, and, by the way, in tithing to my church. "Those who give to the poor will lack nothing, but those who close their eyes to them receive many curses."

Proverbs 30:7–9, raises the stakes a bit to something more monumental, to the entire subject of poor and the rich. Which would you rather be? Be honest here. All things considered, wouldn't you rather be rich? But listen to the God-given prayer of the writer of Proverbs.

> Two things I ask of you, Lord;
> do not refuse me before I die:
> Keep falsehood and lies far from me;
> *give me neither poverty nor riches*, [emphasis added]
> but give me only my daily bread.
> Otherwise, I may have too much and disown you
> and say, "Who is the Lord?"
> Or I may become poor and steal,
> and so dishonor the name of my God.

What we *can* understand, take in, meditate on, and believe in is that, as we read and study these passages, we begin to understand these truths in the light of God's will to do his bidding, with the clear understanding that he will take care of every last one of us walking in his will, regardless of the circumstances.

Questions for Discussion:

- What are some of the "hard truths" described in this chapter? Does Scripture mince words or hold back in describing the rich and poor in the Bible? Give some examples.

- Why was the poor servant in the parable of the talents apparently treated so shabbily by the returning master? What five lessons can we draw from this parable?

- What *are* some hard truths in your life, especially related to work and wealth?

?campaign=11935159&gclid=CjgKEAjwzcWcBRCat43fy9e5i3ASJADXOBwuIqwpz5E4
LK3-GCDbo7p-8Pt9lJFs7HpVlHOgO6e2VPD_BwE.

8

A Very Sad Story

Dear Abby:

My husband, "Simon," is a workaholic. I didn't know him long before I married him, which was a mistake. He never adapted to being part of a couple. His rewards all came from work—the paychecks, kudos from clients and fellow employees, and others saying what a good provider he was. He bought our kids love with presents, not [his] presence.

He was [often] gone, came home after the kids were in bed, volunteered to work on his "off" days [and] usually stayed later [at work] than scheduled. He kept busy with everyone and everything except us. I raised our children alone and worked outside the home as well. I took them to their sports events, extra activities, and to the synagogue. We didn't need the "extra" money, but he was never satisfied, always wanting more. I was faithful to a ghost, living alone and crying for too long. After 30 years, I realized I didn't miss him anymore. He had broken my heart and fractured my dreams.

It's too late for me to start again and find love, Abby. Tell young wives to trust their hearts and priorities. They deserve warmth, not cold cash.

Signed: *Alone now by choice in Pennsylvania*

THE ABOVE APPEARED IN the Dear Abby column in my hometown newspaper, *The Tuscaloosa News*, on Saturday, March 17, 2012.

What does it say to us, contemplating the subject of work and wealth in the Bible? How does one work and enjoy the fruit of one's work without work "taking over" and becoming, as the husband described above, a "workaholic," or one consumed by work that has become addictive, like an alcoholic with alcohol and a drug addict to drugs? How many people do you hurt when you do nothing but satisfy yourself?

And how satisfying is work in today's world anyhow? Apparently, it is just as frustrating and unsatisfying at it was to the author of Ecclesiastes who wrote over 2000 years ago:

> I undertook great projects: I built houses for myself and planted vineyards. I made gardens and parks and planted all kinds of fruit trees in them. I made reservoirs to water groves of flourishing trees. I bought male and female slaves and had other slaves who were born in my house. I also owned more herds and flocks than anyone in Jerusalem before me. I amassed silver and gold for myself, and the treasure of kings and provinces. I acquired male and female singers, and a harem as well—the delights of a man's heart. I became greater by far than anyone in Jerusalem before me. In all this my wisdom stayed with me.
>
> I denied myself nothing my eyes desired;
> I refused my heart no pleasure.
> My heart took delight in all my labor,
> and this was the reward for all my toil.
> Yet when I surveyed all that my hands had done
> and what I had toiled to achieve,
> everything was meaningless, a chasing after the wind;
> nothing was gained under the sun.[1]

Hugh Welchel summarized that "at the close of the twentieth century, during the height of rampant materialism, work was seen only as a means to an end," a "chasing after the wind," as the author of Ecclesiastes, probably King Solomon, wrote in frustration.[2] Today, as young people in their twenties enter the work force, "many are filled with feelings of anxiety and failure."[3] Their high expectations are dashed by the reality of working. When pollsters and commentators have taken the pulse of Generation Y (twenty-somethings) they "found that most people's number-one fear is having lived a meaningless life."[4] It's not that they are misguided and selfish, since a recent

---

1. Eccl 2:4–11.

2. Welchel, *How Then Should We Work*, 109.

3. Ibid.

4. Ibid., 110, drawing on Richard Leider and David Shapiro, *Repacking Your Bags: Lighten Your Load for the Rest of Your Life.*

Harris Poll found that a "monumental 97% of Generation Y . . . are looking for work which allows them to have an impact on the world."[5]

What about older people? Ahem, I am an "older" person, am "retired," but I still work. I *need* to work. In an article in *U.S. News* in 2014, Tom Sightings, a former publishing executive who was "eased into retirement" in his fifties wrote about the needs of people who can and do retire early. It's not so simple, a lifelong trip to the mountains, the beach, or on a cruise on your sailboat through the islands of the Caribbean for the next five years.[6] Or what about just playing golf or puttering around the garden. How long can you do those before you are bored to tears? Where is the satisfaction?

Sightings stays engaged, or working, and he suggests three reasons older people should consider before kicking back into the world of leisure.

1. You need the money

2. You like what you do

3. You have no other interests

He explores each one of these, but number 2 is what interest us. Sightings writes, even if you are financially able to retire,

> Is that what you want to do? Don't underestimate the daily routine you've established over the years—the morning coffee on the way to work, the lunches you enjoy with colleagues and the after-work softball league. *Think about your actual work. Do you enjoy the challenge give-and-take and feeling of accomplishment when you've completed a project?* [emphasis added]. And, what about your identity? Are you proud to be a lawyer, accountant, carpenter, chef or whatever else you may be? A lot of people find self-worth in what they do. Are you ready to be lumped in with the AARP crowd that is simply retired?[7]

What is missing from Sightings article is provided for in Hugh Welchel's very useful little book, *How Then Should We Work?* Welchel writes very directly that "the purpose of this book is to explore the Biblical intersection of faith and work, attempting to understand the differences

---

5. Ibid., 110, drawing on David Bornstein, *How to Change the World: Social Entrepreneurs and the Power of New Ideas.*

6. Sightings, "The Downside of Early Retirement."

7. Ibid.

between work, calling, and vocation and how they should be Biblically applied in our daily lives."[8]

Welchel brings together one's faith and one's work—in largely a modern context—and how they need to be of one piece, rather than two parts of our lives.

He quotes from a very revealing and honest confession by Michael P. Schutt, in his book *Redeeming Law*. Schutt, a young lawyer is trying to reconcile his faith with his work. "We wanted to be more than Christians muddling through the law," Schutt writes. "We wanted to be Christian lawyers, our faith integrated with our calling. We found little guidance in the classroom [not unsurprisingly], from our texts, or from practicing lawyers and professors. Or from [he adds kind of wistfully] from our pastors and priests."[9] We return in the final chapter below, "In God We Trust," to consider the views portrayed so well by Welchel and others—that work needs always to be part of our total view of how we fit into God's plans. The monks of the Middle Ages would have well understood Welchel.

The Apostle Paul addresses the issue indirectly. In other words, if I have to make my work part of my Christian walk, can I choose to do so? Or, am I a slave to circumstances—birth, poverty, genes, etc.—that I cannot change?

Paul, in another context but with the same principle that I wish to underscore here, wrote to the church at Corinth, which was having problems in determining what was permitted and what was not, "'I have the right to do anything,' you say—but not everything [Paul responds] is beneficial. 'I have the right to do anything'—but I will not be mastered by anything" (1 Cor 6:12). Paul was actually writing of a number of sins and excesses, but the principle he invokes is that while he has the liberty to do anything, thereby recalling the principle of free will, not everything is good.

One has to choose every day, and Paul clearly states there is accountability in making wrong choices. "Neither the sexually immoral nor idolaters nor adulterers nor men who have sex with men nor thieves nor the greedy nor drunkards nor slanderers nor swindlers will inherit the kingdom of God" (1 Cor 6:10–11). Basically he puts those absorbed by greed and satisfying their self-gratifying needs into the same category of thieves, drunkards, slanderers, homosexuals, and swindlers, and the implications are clear: they will not inherit the kingdom of God.

8. Welchel, *How Then Should We Work?*, 5.

9. Ibid., 4, quoting from Michael P. Schutt, *Redeeming Law: Christian Calling and the Legal Profession*.

While we are dealing with greed and wealth acquisition in this short chapter, at stake is one of the biggest issues in Christianity: free will versus predestination or the absolute sovereignty of God which we considered in chapter 4 above on the Puritans. Or, to recall, does one have free will, or is one born predestined to be saved, or, conversely, not to be saved? The principle of free will is stated very explicitly in not only the New Testament but also in the Old.

"See, I am setting before you today a blessing and a curse," the chronicler—usually attributed to Moses—of Deuteronomy writes. "The blessing if you obey the commands of the Lord your God that I am giving you today; the curse if you disobey the commands of the Lord your God and turn from the way that I command you today by following other gods, which you have not known" (Deut 11: 26–28). "Other gods" has always included wealth and riches which displace God in your life, such as what happens to produce a workaholic.

Returning to our theme of this short chapter, in Revelation, John writes with clarity on the significance of being wealthy or rich, such as the husband described in the epigraph at the opening of this chapter. "You say, 'I am rich; I have acquired wealth and do not need a thing.' But you do not realize that you are wretched, pitiful, poor, blind and naked. I counsel you to buy from me gold refined in the fire, so you can become rich; and white clothes to wear, so you can cover your shameful nakedness; and salve to put on your eyes, so you can see" (Rev 3:17–18). There are a number of images in the lines above that you can look up in any good commentary on the book of Revelation, but we won't pursue that right now. What John wrote was remarkably clear and almost a perfect summation of the materialistic society such as we inhabit today in the U.S., or reflects on the materialism of other advanced, industrial and post-industrial societies.

As we move to the final chapter on trusting God, we are reminded of the goal of this little book: to teach us what Scripture—God's word—tells us on work and wealth, and, equally important, how to put those principles and instructions to work (sorry for the pun) in our lives. In the final chapter that follows, "In God We Trust," we indirectly push work and wealth aside momentarily, and turn to the guiding principle that God fulfills all our needs and desires. We never abandon the reality that we still live in this world, and God sees to our needs (resources to live, and, sometimes, wealth) and provides for our joy and happiness (our work) in everything we do.

Questions for Discussion:

- What's the "sad story" in this chapter?

- Are you satisfied in your work?

- If not, what do you need to do to get in God's will with respect to work?

9

In God We Trust

Whoever gives heed to instruction prospers,
and blessed is the one who *trusts in the Lord*
(Prov 16:20).

Many are the woes of the wicked,
but the Lord's unfailing love
surrounds the one *who trusts in him* (Prov 32:10).

Blessed is the one
who *trusts in the Lord*,
who does not look to the proud,
to those who turn aside to false gods (Prov 40:4).

LET'S TAKE A LOOK at one of the fundamental principles that this country was founded upon. "In God We Trust." Everyone is familiar with that phrase, at least if you are an American. It is part of your heritage.

Did you know it is the official national motto of the United States?

And of the State of Florida for added measure?

You may not subscribe to it. You may be an atheist or an agnostic, or a Muslim, Buddhist, or Santero, but, in fact, it is a principle written into the cornerstone of the foundations of the nation.

And it does not refer to any other god other than the Judeo-Christian God of the Bible.

Notice that it does not say "In Gold We Trust," or "In Ourselves We Trust," or "In Work We Trust," or anything else you'd like to substitute. It says "In God We Trust," and so as we near the end of this little primer on work and wealth we return also to the source of our wealth and prosperity, God.

It is perhaps ironic that the one element that causes us so many problems—wealth—comes directly from God as a gift. Even more specifically,

God does not bestow wealth or provide for us like a win in lotto, but rather he gives us the wherewithal to live within his Word, and it is his desire that we prosper if we stay in his will.

Secondarily, it is, as by now you know if you have read this far, not the nature of the gift that causes us problems and grief, but what we *do* with that gift.

The origins of "In God We Trust" certainly lays with our Puritan forbearers, more specifically the colony of Massachusetts founded by a small group of Puritans in 1630 and led by John Winthrop. As we have seen above, Edmund S. Morgan's *The Puritan Dilemma: the Story of John Winthrop* is a thoughtful, immensely well-informed study of the Puritans and their migration from England and first few decades in New England.

As Morgan wrote, "Puritanism meant many things . . . but to young John Winthrop it principally meant the problem of living in this world without taking his mind off God."[1] Or, stated another way, Puritans lived in a sinful world, in which they themselves were sinners, but were enjoined and commanded by God to refrain from sin, even though they would sin anyhow. Or, even another way of describing the Puritan, this time with a view toward work as we have been doing in this book: "Puritanism required that he *work* to the best of his ability at whatever task was set before him and partake of the good things that God had filled the world with but told him he must enjoy his work and his pleasures only, as it were, absent-mindedly, with his attention fixed on God."[2]

That was the core of the Puritan dilemma. How to live and do good in a world where Satan ruled and evil prevailed. Secondarily, but no less important, was the Puritan's general belief in predestination, or that God had predestined some to eternal salvation, and others not. Puritans were never altogether certain which category God had assigned them to, and since God was sovereign, he could do as he please.

Confounding and contradicting, it would seem, the doctrine of predestination was the one of free will. God had endowed man with a free will to determine whether he would decide to abide by God's ordinances and commandments, or do as *he* pleases, which he could choose to do. We dealt with free will in the chapter immediately above.

We dealt with predestination in another section of this book, but the Puritans in the main tended to adhere to predestination. But they didn't all

1. Morgan, *Puritan Dilemma*, 8.
2. Ibid., italics added.

WEALTH AND WORK IN SCRIPTURE

go around joylessly looking for someone to condemn and so condemned the term "Puritan" to a cliché for a self-righteous, gloomy, humorless lot. H. L. Mencken sarcastically defined Puritanism as "the haunting fear that someone, somewhere, may be happy."

The truth is not with Mencken's wit, but with Winthrop's life. As Morgan described it, Winthrop took pleasure in a number of areas. He was married several times as wives passed away with frightening regularity, but the one who lived the longest, his beloved Margaret, was a close and loving companion and they enjoyed each other's company as God meant for a man and woman. Winthrop also loved to hunt, but he sometimes anguished over it since it was distracting from his godly time, and, besides, as his biographer Morgan noted, Winthrop was a poor shot and was as much frustrated as satisfied with the hunt.

Winthrop loved to work, and the Puritans bequeathed this to the making of this nation. "Above all else, he had learned to stick to business. If he worked hard at whatever task lay before him, he could take his pleasures in stride."[3]

And Morgan noted one problem all who love work have faced. "Of course work itself could be a snare," as we explored in chapter 6 above. "It was easy to become engrossed in it for its own sake or for the sake of the worldly goods it brought. A man who labored merely for gain, with no thought for God, was no better than a libertine."[4] At every point of his life, Winthrop paused and checked to see if he was in step with God.

As we consider work and wealth in this long essay/little book, that's not a principle to be cast aside as the workings of an overzealous and joyless Puritan. It is taking the only true measurement of truth and wisdom— found in Scripture—and using it as your guide. To do otherwise is to trust in man's wisdom, and, if not inspired by God and given a form that reflects God's mandates, commandments, and especially the teachings of Jesus, then the outcome will be perishable and useless in your walk as a Christian.

Sorry, that's a bit of preaching, but, let's recall, we are searching for and analyzing what the Bible has to say about work and wealth, and as it becomes obvious on what it does say, then we need to put it into practice. See my *Cleared for Landing: On Living a Christian Life* for how to put Christian principles to work in your life, where practice, practice, practice is the key.

3. Ibid., 11.
4. Ibid.

God, by the way, if this hasn't become absolutely and perfectly clear by now, not only approves of a hard-working man, but also commands it. As Morgan noted, "but he [like Winthrop] who worked because God willed it, multiplying his talents like a good and faithful servant, could throw himself into his job almost as a way of worship, without fear of losing balance. That he might amass a fortune in the process was an incidental benefit, not be treated as a goal, but not to be rejected if it came."[5]

Winthrop was a noticeably conscientious worker and "apparently had no difficulty in maintaining the right attitude to his work."[6] While work did not define Winthrop or the Puritans, the results of work—success or failure—were seen as evidence of God's hand on, or off, of them. Winthrop was keen on measuring and weighing the results of his efforts. "Just as Winthrop considered hunting with a gun a bad form of recreation because he got so little profit from it, so the move to New England was wrong unless there was a good chance that the colony would be an economic success."[7] Failure was not God's providential hand at work.

God's hand was *always* at work here. "A man's duty to God was to work at his calling and improve his talents like a good and faithful servant," recalling of course the parable by the same name in Matt 25:14–30 (ESV), sometimes also called the parable of the talents or the parable of the bags of gold. It is, actually, one of Jesus' fundamental parables that directly addresses both wealth and work in the same story. The significance of that parable was explained in chapter 7 above.

Winthrop never took his eyes off of his God for very long. "God was the overwhelming reality, indeed the only reality," Morgan emphasized. "Success and failure were relevant only as *indications*, and not always reliable ones, of His satisfaction or displeasure with a man's efforts to serve Him as he passed through life."[8]

It is sometimes hard to imagine such a godly society, or one so devoted to doing God's will, so well described by the title to this chapter, "In God We Trust." Morgan noted that "the Puritans did make strong demands on human nature, for they were engaged in a mission that required great

---

5. Ibid.
6. Ibid., 14.
7. Ibid., 35.
8. Ibid., 39, italics added.

exertions. They had undertaken to establish a society where the will of God would be observed in every detail, a kingdom of God on earth."[9]

By today's standards, they were religious zealots bent on forcing all to conform, in a land where eventually freedom of the individual would be extolled and even made the subject of the first ten amendments to the Constitution, the Bill of Rights. But the Puritans did not confuse freedom with rights. They had certain rights as Englishmen, given definition by charters and common law, but the only freedom allowed in the new colony, a city on a hill, a beacon to the true believers, was the freedom to obey God.

However, there was often a fine line between what was "sin and mere temptation or between sin and simple human pleasure." The line was a thin one but Winthrop "knew that the line must be firmly drawn, for it would be as wrong to forbid what God allowed as it would be to allow what He forbade"[10] The use of alcohol was a good example of how to tread this fine line.

They knew that liquor—largely beer and wine in the Bible—"was one of the good things that God has furnished His people for their comfort, nourishment, and recreation."[11] That's good news for Presbyterians, Episcopalians, Roman Catholics, and other who enjoy the fruit of the vine occasionally, in or out of church services. The Puritans would have approved. But "drunkenness . . . was wrong, and the Puritans punished it without hesitation . . . The path from drink to drunkenness was so short and easy that they found it hard to decide whether any barriers should be placed along it."[12] Baptists and others who don't touch the stuff would approve of the latter. Puritans tried to remove some temptations, like forbidding people to drink toasts to one another. And good Puritans that they were, they debated this issue hotly since they were "forbidding a temptation rather than a sin," and so going beyond God's commission.[13]

It is a useful debate to consider, since regulations on wealth and work—at least in the Puritan framework of building God's kingdom on earth—had to conform to or reflect God's ordinances. Winthrop's friend Thomas Shepard, the minister of the church at Cambridge, pointed out this flawed thinking to the governor. "The law," said Shepard in a letter to Winthrop,

9. Ibid., 69.

10. Ibid., 71–72.

11. Ibid., 72.

12. Ibid., 63.

13. Ibid.

was all wrong. By treating a temptation as a sin, it would provoke God, for this was making "more sins than (as yet is seene) God himself hath made."[14]

The Puritans firmly believed in the title of this chapter, "In God We Trust," and they certainly tried to put their lives in the order God desired and expressed in Scripture. We have focused on work and wealth, since that is the theme of this essay, but the Puritans looked at *everything* in their lives as subject to, and to be measured against, the will of God.

Today, we, of course, are not Puritans. Almost four hundred years of history have passed since that day in 1630 when they stepped ashore from the *Arbella* and began their grand experiment to establish God's kingdom on earth. To them God had provided for pleasure *and* fulfillment in work, and even in the acquisition of wealth. This latter really came later as their colony took root and began to develop an industry based on the export of lumber, foods, grains, fish, and other products of the land and surrounding seas to places in the Atlantic world, all the way from the English colonies to the south, in the Caribbean, and even to the Spanish and Portuguese islands and possessions far across the oceans.

I think most of us fall into three camps when it comes to the Puritan legacy, even if you never knew anything about the Puritans until you read some of the chapters above.

Either you:

- accept their general premises based on God's will as expressed in Scripture,
- you reject it entirely as the neurosis of a stiff-necked, self-righteous people who thought only they had the knowledge to truth and power,
- or, you fall somewhere in the middle, admitting the truth of their position, but modifying it to accommodate a nation that developed on toleration and freedom of will.

Our Declaration of Independence, after all, championed the right of all people to "life, liberty, and the pursuit of happiness." John Winthrop would probably have approved of that felicitous summation by Thomas Jefferson of one of the central truths that underlay the American Revolution, but Winthrop would have added "consistent with God's will," although I am certain he would have expressed it in far more elegant terms.

14. Ibid.

For the Puritans there also existed the reality that some were predestined to wealth and power, and some to be poor. As Winthrop expressed it (the epigraph for chapter 5 above), that "God Almightie in his most holy and wise providence hath soe disposed of the Condicion of mankind, as in all times some must be rich some poore, some highe and eminent in power and dignitie; others meane and in subjeccion."[15]

He wasn't being cruel in expressing these sentiments, just following Scripture that not only expressed God's will but also expressed the reality of the world. We explored some of these in the preceding chapter, "Some Very Hard Truths." See Proverbs 22, for examples, of the expression of these realities.

> The rich rule over the poor,
> and the borrower is slave to the lender (Prov 22:7).
> Rich and poor have this in common:
> The LORD is the Maker of them all (Prov 22:2).

Is the whole world, rather fatalistically, divided between rich and poor? That is a question that needs another book, one based on the Christian legacy measured against and within modern political sentiments.

The first expression of this new political philosophy was the American Revolution, based on the liberty and rights of *all* individuals. There were to be no peasants and kings in this new republic. All were created equal. What they *did* with this privilege is of course another story. Some grasped it and strode out in front of others. Some were followers.

A well-defined society emerged—not classed by blood lines or privileges defined by inherited prominence (nobles, kings, peasants, etc.)—but one defined mostly by wealth and power accumulated in an increasingly capitalist society. The rich were *really* rich, and the poor, industrialized, working classes often were *really* poor and/or little more than cogs in the wheels of industrialization and urbanization that defined the modern world. However, over time, an emerging middle class—smaller entrepreneurs, bureaucrats, professionals, farmers, ranchers, and dozens of other categories—rose to dominate the class scene in our country, and eventually produced a society where the extremes of wealth and poverty were small in comparison to the middle class, and the stability it gave to the nation.

The most powerful response to the rise of capitalism, as we saw in an earlier chapter, was Marxism or socialism in the nineteenth and twentieth

15. Ibid., 88.

centuries. Communism championed the leveling of society and rigidly followed the "rules" of capitalism as given definition by Marx and his followers. God did not play much of a role in Marxism, other than being denigrated as the "opiate of the masses" by Marx. He viewed Christianity as deflecting the legitimate aspirations of the growing working classes by requiring obedience in this world, and so being rewarded in the next. Or, be a good man and obey your bosses and leaders and God will take care of you for eternity. That, of course, was in the next life, not this one. In this one, be a good and obedient servant or worker. Ergo, the "opiate" of the masses.

But godless Marxism and Communism went bankrupt in the twentieth century when it was tried and tested on a massive basis in places like Russia, China, Cuba, and others. There has to be another solution to the problems created by work and wealth, poverty and riches, in the modern world.

This leads us back to Paul, when writing to the Corinthians, about free choices. "'I have the right to do anything,' you say—but not everything is beneficial. 'I have the right to do anything'—but I will not be mastered by anything" (1Cor 6:12).

While this instruction by Paul is in the context of Paul discussing sexual immorality, it is just as valid for choosing between what Scripture says and admonishes us about wealth and work, or choosing to follow the dictates and whims of the world we live in.

And, returning to the theme and title of this chapter, "In God We Trust," if we really believe that, then we need to act on it. We need to be obedient to God's will and obedient with respect to work and wealth. Do that and God will provide—always—a felicitous life for you.

Now, modern man (we all think we're modern; even the Romans considered themselves modern when measuring their civilization against the barbarians, for example), has tended to separate work from faith.

A simple example helps to illustrate this phenomenon. We go to church on Sundays, maybe attend Sunday School, and assume a public role of piety and obedience to the Lord. But for the rest of the week, the other six days, we put obedience to God, love of the Lord, love of our neighbor, we put most of that aside and get on with the "real world"—our work. And during our leisure or off-work time, we head to the golf course, the tennis courts, the gym, the lake, the shore (for you New Jersey readers), the stadium, or someplace else—all of this can be wholesome and good for you—but it does not relate to our Sunday "church" persona.

I know the above is harsh, and probably many of you (I hope there are many of you reading this, making my venture into publishing capitalism good for me!) are more godly in your lives than the person or people I just described in the paragraph above. But I suspect there is some of the above in all of us. We separate work from faith.[16]

This is where Hugh Welchel's book *How Then Should We Work?* is very helpful. He focuses his book on something called *vocational calling*, or the work we do in the world, or even more simply put, our work.[17] And to understand his point of view, it is useful to understand our work as a form of "calling" as a Christian. We are called, like the apostles were, to become followers of Jesus, and Welchel and others—especially Reformation giants like Martin Luther and John Calvin—extended the nature of "calling" to include everything we do, including our work. Personally, I don't think Luther, Calvin, and others were pioneering such a radical departure from what the Apostle Paul, fifteen hundred years before them, considered his "calling" to be. See for example: "Paul, a servant of Christ Jesus, called to be an apostle and set apart for the gospel of God" (Rom 1:1). Paul, a close student of Judaism, a tentmaker by profession, and called by Jesus to be the apostle to the Gentiles, did not separate his life—tentmaker, apostle, teacher, evangelist, etc.—into separate and distinct parts of his life. It was all one calling. Work and being called to be a Christian were but two parts of the whole. As the Paul expressed it so felicitously, "So whether you eat or drink or whatever you do, do it all for the glory of God."[18] But, in today's world, as Welchel describes it so well in his chapter 4, "Our Current Situation," there tends to be a radical disconnect between work and church.

William Diehl describes the frustration of this failed connection between his work and his faith. "In the almost thirty years of my professional career [a Bethlehem Steel executive]," he writes, "my church has never once suggested that there by any type of accounting of my on-the-job ministry to others. My church has never once offered to improve these [ministerial] skills, which could make me a better [lay] minister . . . There has never been

16. Well described in an episode in Welchel, *How Then Should We Work?*, 79, quoting from Laura L. Nash, Ken Blanchard, and Scotty McLennan, *Church on Sunday, Work on Monday: The Challenge of Fusing Christian Values with Business Life.*

17. Welchel, to give him his due, does separate work into a number of distinct categories like primary calling, secondary calling, etc. but they are largely musings—and useful—with more of a theological bent.

18. 1 Cor 10:31.

an inquiry into the types of ethical decisions I must face, or whether I seek to communicate my faith to my coworkers."

And less one church or denomination be the target of this sad, and delinquent on the part the church, commentary, Diehl adds

> I have never been in a congregation where there was any type of public affirmation of a ministry in my career. In short, I must conclude that my church doesn't have the least interest whether or how I minister in my daily work.[19]

I must add that in my church this is not a subject tiptoed around. We are all called to be ministers of our faith, in one fashion or another, and if we take the call from the pulpit seriously, then this obviously carries into work life outside of the church. But the link between work and faith is often not made explicitly.

Welchel notes, very correctly, that "the integration of faith and work is misunderstood not only by the church members who sit in the pews but by those who stand behind the pulpit."

"Our vocation," he explains, "should be 'an element of Christian discipleship, a habit of the mind and heart of listening for and responding to the voice of the Lord,' yet this concept is missing from most churches."[20]

How do we describe ourselves when first introduced, or what do we first ask of a stranger?

"What do you do?" [by which] we mean, "What is your job?"[21] Our career defines us in contemporary society. In some societies, it is impolite to be so direct as to ask people what they do. Even in our rather direct way of dealing with people in our culture, we sometimes tiptoe indirectly into the question. What *do* you do?

Hardly anyone will answer, "I am a Christian who works as an engineer, a lawyer, a teacher, a carpenter, a whatever." It would seem presumptuous of us, like trying to convert or evangelize who we are speaking to.

So, we answer, honestly and in keeping with our culture, "I am a [fill in the blank]." Our careers, not our faith, defines us. We dealt with this in chapter 2 above, "What Do You Do?"

And we end this chapter with the same question, "what do you do?" And follow it with the title of the chapter, "In God We Trust."

19. Welchel, *How Then Should We Work?*, 71, quoting from R. Paul Stevens, *The Other Six Days: Vocation, Work, and Ministry in Biblical Perspective*.

20. Ibid., 71–72, quoting from Tim McConnell, "Vocation as Sustained Discipleship."

21. Ibid., 73.

Or, we trust in God to define us, to guide us, to show us, and, in the case of this short book, to do all of those with respect to work and wealth.

Questions for Discussion:

- Review question: what was the Puritan dilemma?

- Hint: what is predestination? Presbyterians have to wait for other denominations to give it their best shot first.

- What are some examples of separating our work from our faith?

- How do Welchel and other students of work, wealth, and Scripture define "calling?"

Conclusion

THIS CONCLUDES OUR SHORT trip through Scripture and what it has to say about work and wealth. In my ignorance of the subject, I thought I could write a short synopsis of the major scriptural passages on work and wealth when I started this project in 2008.

I thought, well I read the Bible every day. I'll just take notes whenever I hit a passage that has to do, in one form or another, with work and wealth. When my notes passed the seventy to eighty page mark, I began to realize the enormity of the subject. And when I started to investigate the secondary literature—what others had written about it—I almost submerged and sank out of sight. What I thought could be a Sunday School primer, or, even better, a guide for politicians and voters alike in forthcoming elections to determine the future of our country, turned out to be my own journey into my faith as a Christian, and my life as an American.

I discovered, for example, a huge literature on the elements of the modern world, such as consumerism, leisure time, technology, and the like, all of which impinge on and have refashioned the relationship of man and work in the past 200 years.

The past beyond that, 1000 or 2000 or 3000 years ago, I handled with a bit more agility, being a professional historian by training. But I was still almost overwhelmed by those who have thought about and written about these subjects over the centuries.

At the heart of this story, the message is that Scripture, the Bible, is very specific on how to handle two of the most fundamental challenges for all humankind, but especially focusing on men and their traditional roles as provider and protector of the family unit, a nice phrase I borrowed from modern sociologists.

In today's overheated but essential political debates on the nature of this country and how men should organize it, work and wealth play immense, perhaps the most important, roles in determining where political leaders stand on how the country should be governed.

We, as a people and country, are not so advanced, not so technologically proficient, not so smart as to have absolved ourselves of the need to work to fulfill God's will in our lives. We have not totally abandoned work for leisure, nor have we capitulated to the robots and drones as substitutes for work, no matter how different "work" is defined in today's, or tomorrow's, world. It is certainly not the plowman of the Middle Ages, or the Roman farmer-soldier of ancient times, but work is nonetheless absolutely essential to defining and claiming your worth in a difficult and complicated world.

So, with some of the above in mind, we—to get the imagination flowing—started, not at the beginning, but with a rather whimsical and invented interview between some smart media people and Jesus Christ and the Apostle Paul. In it Jesus and Paul explained some of the "rules" for work, and, if you earned it, what to do with wealth. This short interview serves to introduce you to the basis for the entire premise of this book: the fundamental principles for working and wealth are in the Bible and one must search, and then interpret, those principles and apply them to the specific situation, or problem, or challenge of the moment.

A quick for example: what do I do with an abundance of riches (determined by many different ways, from old fashioned land holding to modern paper equities) that I have accumulated or inherited, or both? This is not a fictitious or imagined circumstance. Many of us face it every day. It is real.

Or, a second example: I hate my work, I hate my boss, and I am in a dead end job with no promise or hope of advancement ahead of me. This too is not fictitious or imagined. Millions of people find themselves as described above, with different details and circumstances obviously, but stuck in an apparently ceaseless cycle of unhappiness and often desperation. What to do?

In chapters 2 and 3 we explored what is it about certain work that is satisfying and other that is merely self-serving. We returned to Scripture, and especially to certain of the parables of Jesus, so simply presented yet with such profound lessons, on what is important—after all is said and done—in life.

If there is a "heart" to this little book, it is probably taken together, chapters 4 and 6.

Chapter 4 starts with a very controversial modern theological premise—summed up in the catchy "Name It and Claim It" philosophy—and explores the power of wealth to undermine our relationship with God, finishing with a strong section on the Puritans and their dilemma. Their dilemma is an ageless one for Christians, and is still just as prevalent in our lives today as it was for Puritans almost four hundred years ago and for Roman Christians a millennium ago: how to know you are saved, and, two, how gain admission to that privileged group of the saved. If you have read closely, you will be obviously aware of the trap of wealth and work in the unending relationship of man and his God. One cannot "work" oneself into the forgiving salvation offered by Jesus, but working—at a living—is fundamental to our lives.

It is my contention that the nature of work and the disposition of wealth are two fundamental factors in how the country came to be what it was, and, equally important, what it should be now and in the future.

Chapter 5, "Work and the Protestant Work Ethic" addresses the question: is work a means or an end? Or, framed another way, *why* do we work? The answer is both in the life and history of the Puritans which is examined fairly closely in this chapter, and in the "Protestant work ethic" which spun off from the Puritan experience with trying to live by Scripture in a world most decidedly *not* governed by Scripture. Or, how can we live like God wants us to live when we are drawn away from God by everything around us, even including ourselves more than occasionally? Or, as the Apostle Paul framed it in his letter to the Romans, "I do not understand what I do. For what I want to do I do not do, but what I hate I do."[1]

This chapter also draws from the pioneering work by the modern "father" of sociology, Max Weber, and his pathbreaking *The Protestant Ethic and the Spirit of Capitalism*, often described as the Protestant work ethic. Or, put another way, Weber hypothesized, and then went on to prove his hypothesis, that the desire and will to work—especially by the Puritans—underlay the rise of capitalism, which so transformed the world in the past three centuries. To the Puritans, work was not simply an expression of God's will, but a transformative experience whose product—wealth and prosperity—could be interpreted as proof of God's salvation. This is an immensely controversial aspect of soteriology, or the study of salvation across religions, and you will profitably read both in chapter 4 ("Name It and Claim It") and chapter 5 ("Work and the Protestant Work Ethic") how Puritan concepts and doctrines underlay not only the Protestant religious foundations of this country, but also were woven into the very fabric of the political theories—especially emphasizing liberty and freedom—that underlay the making of the American Revolution, and, later, the Constitution.

1. Rom 7:15.

We still argue and debate *freedom* versus *equality* in this country, for example—both principles integrated foundationally into the Declaration of Independence and the Constitution. And, as explained in chapters 4 and 5, for wealth creation, or capitalism, to have flourished, it needed to do so in an environment of economic and political liberty, which leads us to the next chapter.

Chapter 6, or "How Work Got to be a Dirty Word," traces the history of how the increasing complexity of societies tended to divide people into different classes and castes and how work contributed to the making of class and social distinctions.

We began in ancient times when work and life were so intertwined that there *was* no word for work. To work was to live, and not to work, to be idle. Idleness, or sloth, was a sin among the ancient Hebrews, in the same category as the "seven deadly sins" of wrath, avarice, sloth, pride, lust, envy, and gluttony so characterized by later Christianity but defined and identified in Scripture.[2] There are various lists of these cardinal sins, but one can easily identify those associated with work and wealth, such as avarice, sloth, pride, envy, and even gluttony. That's five out of seven, not a bad percentage, and good reason to contemplate, with rigor and honesty, what we have done in this little book on work and wealth.

We followed some of the major modern authors in their narrative and analysis of work and wealth, especially the very excellent study of work across the ages by Herbert Applebaum, *The Concept of Work: Ancient, Medieval, and Modern*. Included in this genre was also the excellent study of wealth among early Christians by Justo B. González, *A History of Early Christian Ideas on the Origin, Significance, and Use of Money*.

At the core of this chapter is the evolution of how societies and civilizations gradually belittled and categorized manual labor as less important forms of labor and work, and lifted up those with circumstances (by birth, intelligence, luck, skill, whatever) such as philosophers, warriors, politicians, and even prelates and higher church officials, into a privileged ruling class. By the Middle Ages, a well-established caste system was in place, ruled by kings and nobles, and manned by the thousands and millions of laborers, from the lowest serfs and slaves on the landed estates to the evolving crafts and tradesmen of the latter Middle Ages.

In Christian theory, all were still equal, but, in fact, kings and nobles were thought to have been born to govern and make war, while the rest of

2. Prov 6:16–19; Gal 5:19–21.

humankind worked. Somehow the ancient Hebrew and early Christians' notions of work itself being a noble expression of worshipping God had been subverted.

But while society became more stratified, pockets of Christians, especially within the monastic movement, continued to esteem and extol work and labor. They, in fact, preserved these ancient principles derived from Judaism and early Christianity, although modified somewhat by the monastic life.

There was, as you have read, a constant struggle to reconcile man's determination to impose his will and notions of what was important and what was not important on the scriptural principles on work and wealth that stressed all the virtues you have read about above.

Chapter 7, "Some Very Hard Truths," is devoted to putting together much of what Scripture has to say about wealth. We tend to think of the Bible as hopelessly idealistic, out of tune with the "real" world, filled with pious platitudes and commandments, none of which have much bearing on how the world really works. In fact, as you have read in this chapter, Scripture, especially many passages from the Old Testament, like Proverbs, Psalms, and Ecclesiastes for example, are so candid that they sometimes hurt to read they are so close to the truth. It's kind of like looking into a magic mirror which reflects your real self, not the one you have imagined yourself to be.

But, and this is true (a good truth we'd like to think) for most of what preceded this chapter on "Some Very Hard Truths," we have also laid out how Scripture teaches us to deal with work, and, sometimes more importantly, the wealth that comes our way.

A short chapter 8, "Some Very Hard Choices" looks at the choices we have to make on a daily basis. As in previous chapters, it follows a loose template of not only identifying problems and challenges, but also suggesting the scriptural basis and principles for dealing with the choices.

The last chapter 9, "In God We Trust," returns to John Winthrop and the Puritans, not because they were a likeable lot, but because they struggled with issues that were so enormous that they finally gave up on themselves, and turned to God for answers.

Bibliography

Applebaum, Herbert. *The Concept of Work: Ancient, Medieval, and Modern*. Albany: State University of New York Press, 1992.

Arendt, Hannah. *The Human Condition*. Chicago: University of Chicago Press, 1958.

Augustine. "Of the Blessings with Which the Creator Has Filled This Life, Obnoxious Though it Be to the Curse." In *The City of God*, book 22, chapter 24. New Advent. http://www.newadvent.org/fathers/120122.htm.

Benz, Ernst. *Evolution and Christian Hope: Man's Concept of the Future from the Early Fathers to Teilhard de Chardin*. Garden City, NY: Doubleday, 1966.

Bornstein, David. *How to Change the World: Social Entrepreneurs and the Power of New Ideas*. New York: Oxford University Press, 2007.

Burrawoy, Michael. *Manufacturing Consent: Changes in the Labor Process Under Monopoly Capitalism*. Chicago: University of Chicago Press, 1979.

Clayton, Lawrence. "All Men Are Not Created Equal." *The Tuscaloosa News*. December 24, 2009. http://laclayton.wordpress.com/2009/12/24/hello-world.

———. *Cleared for Landing: On Living a Christian Life*. N.p: Xlibris, 2008.

———. "Religions of the Same Book." *Tuscaloosa News*, November 21, 2010. http://www.tuscaloosanews.com/article/20101121/NEWS/101119554/0/search?p=1&tc=pg.

Dodwell, C. R., ed. and trans. *Introduction to Theophilus: De diversis artibus*. London: Thomas Nelson, 1961.

Donin, Hayim H. *To Be A Jew: A Guide To Jewish Observance In Contemporary Life*. New York: Basic Books, 1972.

Eisenberg, Ronald L. *What the Rabbis Said: 250 Topics from the Talmud*. Santa Barbara, CA: ABC-CLIO, 2010.

Geoghegan, Arthur T. *The Attitude towards Labor in Early Christianity and Ancient Culture*. Washington, DC: The Catholic University of America Press, 1945.

González, Justo B. *Faith and Wealth: A History of Early Christian Ideas on the Origin, Significance, and Use of Money*. Eugene, OR: Wipf & Stock, 2002.

Jacobs, Louis. *The Jewish Religion: A Companion*. New York: Oxford University Press, 1995.

———. "Work in Jewish Thought." My Jewish Learning. N.d. http://www.myjewishlearning.com/practices/Ethics/Business_Ethics/Themes_and_Theology/Value_of_Work.shtml?p=1.

Jellinek, Georg. *The Declaration of the Rights of Man and of Citizens: A Contribution to Modern Constitutional History*. Translated by Max Farrand. New York: Henry Holt, 1901. http://www.gutenberg.org/files/29815/29815-h/29815-h.htm.

Lindsley, Art. "Does the Book of Acts Command Socialism?" The Gospel Coalition. May 28, 2013. http://www.thegospelcoalition.org/article/does-the-book-of-acts-command-socialism/.

Mays, Dorothy A. *Women in Early America: Struggle, Survival, and Freedom in a New World.* Santa Barbara, CA: Clio, 2004.

Morgan, Edmund S. *The Puritan Dilemma: The Story of John Winthrop.* Boston: Little, Brown, 1958.

Nash, Laura L., Ken Blanchard, and Scotty McLennan. *Church on Sunday, Work on Monday: The Challenge of Fusing Christian Values with Business Life.* San Francisco: Jossey-Bass, 2001.

O'Toole, James. *Work in America: Report of a Special Task Force to the Secretary of Health, Education and Welfare.* Cambridge, MA: Massachusetts Institute of Technology Press, 1975.

Roethlisberger, E. J., and W. J. Dickson. *Management and the Worker.* Cambridge, MA: Harvard University Press, 1939.

Schutt, Michael P. *Redeeming Law: Christian Calling and the Legal Profession.* Downers Grove, IL: InterVarsity, 2007.

Sightings, Tom. "The Downside of Early Retirement." *U.S. News and World Report,* December 31, 2013. http://money.usnews.com/money/blogs/on-retirement/2013/12/31/the-downside-of-early-retirement.

Stevens, R. Paul. *The Other Six Days: Vocation, Work, and Ministry in Biblical Perspective.* Grand Rapids: Eerdmans, 2000.

Tawney, R. H. *Religion and the Rise of Capitalism.* New York: Penguin, 1947.

Terkel, Studs. *Working: People Talk About What They Do All Day and How They Feel About What They Do.* New York: Random House, 1972.

Tilgher, Adriano. *Work: What It Has Meant to Men through the Ages.* New York: Harcourt, Brace, 1930.

Troelsch, Ernst. *The Social Teaching of the Christian Church.* Vol. 2 Translated by Olive Wyon. Chicago: University of Chicago Press, 1981.

Warner, Susan, and Gary Anderson. "Putting It On the Line at Mercedes-Benz U.S. International with the Mercedes Production System." Mercedes-Benz Club of America. N.d. http://www.mbca.org/star-article/july-august-2013/putting-it-line-mercedes-benz-us-international-mercedes-production-sys.

Weber, Max. *The Protestant Ethic and the Spirit of Capitalism and Other Writings.* Edited and translated by Peter Baehr and Gordon C. Wells. London: Penguin, 2002.

Welchel, Hugh. "Five Lessons for Our Lives from the Parable of the Talents." Institute for Faith, Work & Economics blog. March 14, 2003. http://blog.tifwe.org/five-lessons-for-our-lives-from-the-parable-of-the-talents.

———. *How Then Should We Work? Rediscovering the Biblical Doctrine of Work.* Bloomington, IN: Westbow, 2012.

Author Index

Applebaum, Herbert, 63–64, 66–70, 82, 84–86, 88–89, 92–94, 96–98, 100, 102, 134, 137
Aquinas, St. Thomas, see subject index for entries
Augustine of Hippo, St., see also subject index, x, 33, 83–86, 137

Benz, Ernst, see also *Evolution and Christian Hope: Man's Concept of the Future from the Early Fathers to Teilhard de Chardin* (book), 86

Calvin, John, 47, 95–97, 99, 104, 128
Cicero, Marcus Tullius, 67–68
Cisterians, 86, 88
Clayton, Lawrence A., see also *Cleared for Landing: On Living a Christian Life* (book), 98, 108, 137
Clement of Alexandria, 75, 83
Cluniacs, 86

Dickins, Charles, 26–27

Franklin, Benjamin, see also *Poor Richard's Almanac* , 48, 97–99, 108

Geoghegan, Arthur T., 69, 137
González, Justo B., see also subject index; *A History of Early Christian Ideas on the Origin, Significance, and Use of Money* (book); 2, 71–73, 76–77, 79–81, 134, 137
Graham, Billy, x

Hananiah, Rabbi Joseph b[en], 70

Jacobs, Rabbi Louis, 61
Jefferson, Thomas, see subject index for entries
Jerome, St., 83

Luther, Martin, see also subject index, 30, 39, 52, 92–95, 98, 103, 128

Marx, Karl, 23, 96, 99–100, 127
Mencken, H. L., 122
Morgan, Edmund, see also subject index, ix, 36–37, 39–40, 53, 109, 121–23, 138

Origin (author), 83
Ovitt, George, see also *The Restoration of Perfection, Labor and Technology in Medieval Culture*, (book), 89

Schutt, Michael P., see also *Redeeming Law* (book), 117, 138
Smith, Adam, see also *Wealth of Nations* (book), 97, 115–116

Tawney, Richard, see also *Religion and the Rise of Capitalism*, (book), 96, 138
Terkel, Studs, see also *Working*, 102
Tertullian, 83
Theophilus, see also *De Diversis Artibus*, 88
Tigher, Adriano, see also *Work and What It Has Meant to Men Through the Ages* (book), 92, 95

Author Index

Troeltsch, Ernst, see also *The Social Teaching of the Christian Church* (book), 97

Weber, Max, ix, 37, 47, 48, 49, 50, 51, 54, 55, 75, 76, 96, 108, 133, 138

Welchel, Hugh, see also *How Then Should We Work* (book), 115–117, 128–130, 138

Winthrop, John, see also subject index; see also Puritans, The; *The Puritan Dilemma*; Puritan dilemma, The, ix, 36, 40, 50–53, 109, 121–126, 135, 138

Subject Index

Scripture Index